Poetic Images: Martha's Vineyard

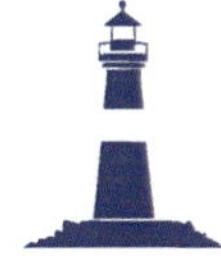

Poems and Photographs by
Bob DiCarlo

POETIC IMAGES PRESS

This is a work of creative nonfiction. Some parts have been fictionalized in varying degrees, for various purposes.

Printed in the United States of America

First Edition, 2024

ISBN 979-8-9900906-0-6

Photography by Bob DiCarlo
Cover image by Bob DiCarlo
Book design by Dimitri LaBarge

Poetic Images Press
86 Gray Street
Amherst, MA 01002

This book is dedicated to the ones that I love - my family and to my friends.

contents

foreword

by Lori DiCarlo Ford

My dad is the funniest, wittiest, most loving family man I know. When he told me he was writing a book with his poems and photographs I was so proud and excited because writing poems and taking pictures was a new art for him. In 2017, he suffered a heart attack which led to a long arduous surgery. Thank you to Dr. Joseph Eugene Flack and his team of nurses from BayState Medical Center in Springfield, MA that saved my dad's life.

Before this life changing event, my dad would write an occasional family newsletter. This was a project far beyond what I had seen him do in the past, but it did not surprise me. My dad has always been a beautiful example of hard work and perseverance. I am grateful to have him as such an amazing role model in my life for me and my children. I know you will feel his love and kindness through his writing and photographs.

introduction

There was this Guy - a Preaching kind of a Man
Who told us that it's better
To Sell - The Sizzle
Lead us by the hand
When you think of an Island
Blue Sky
And all - that Stuff
There's a lot more to it
Than lots of - Fancy Puff
It's more about
That Feeling
Find - Your Happy Place
Yeah - That's it
In a Nut Shell
That's
What - These Poems
Are - Preaching
That's - What It's
All About

island's love

The waves
Hugged me
The embraces
Of the Sun
The touch
Of the Ocean
The scent
Of the wave
Of emotions
That I feel
When I walk
Upon your Sandy Shore
That greets
Morning's Sunshine
Walk in the Rain
Of Love
That I feel
In my heart
Every time
I look into your eyes
My knees shake
With anticipation
My heart beats
Like a drum
I can't get
Enough of you
You - Are
The one
That - I Love

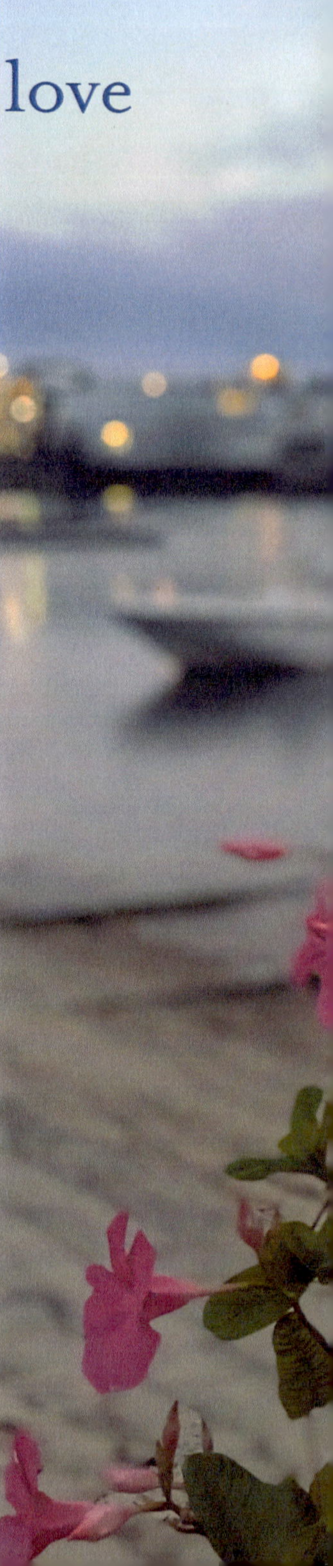

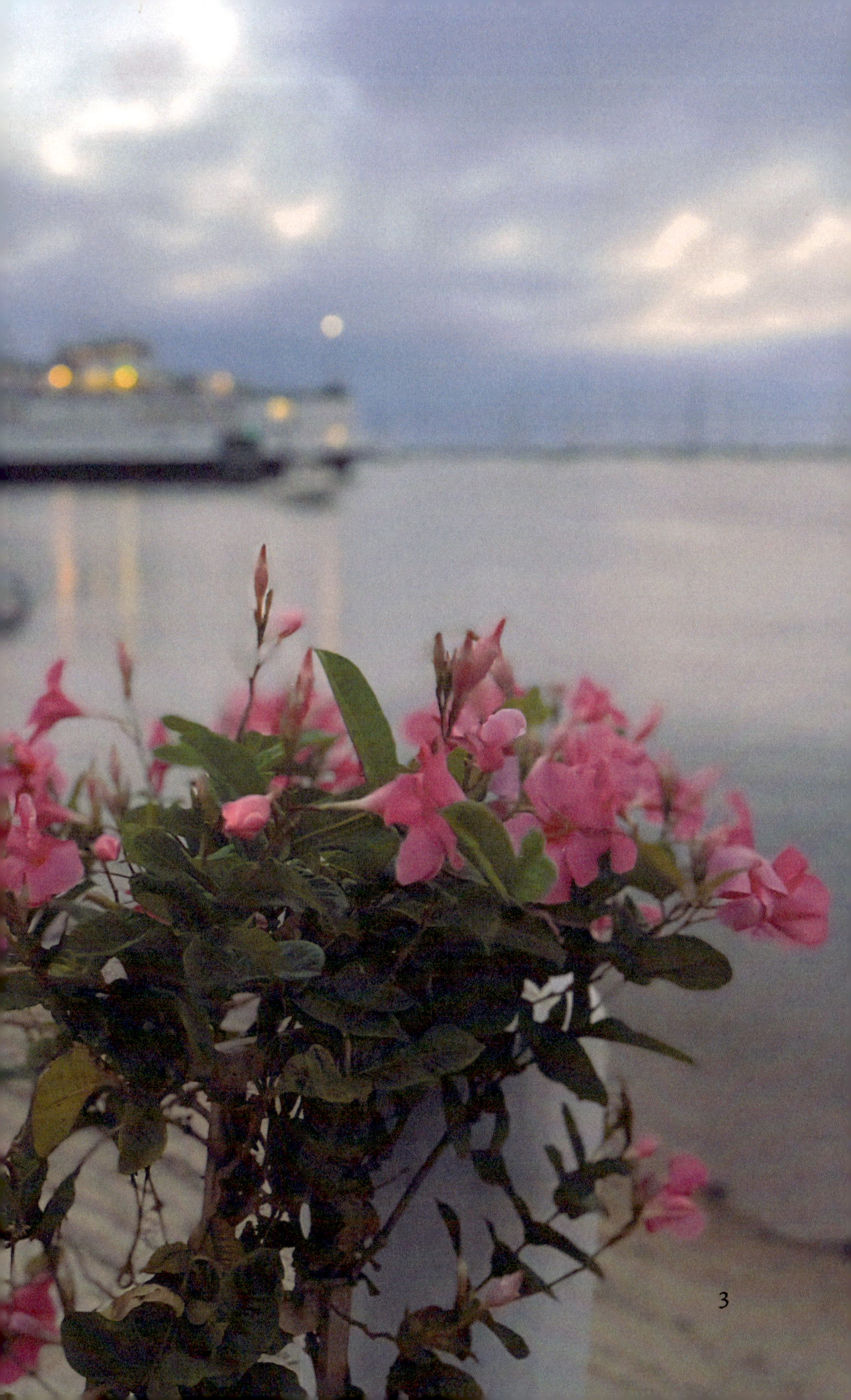

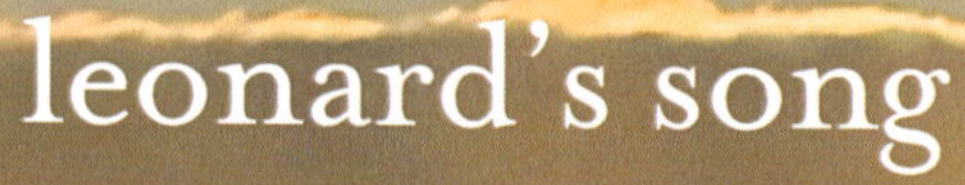

leonard's song

Oh weariness
My head yearns
My soul aches
My heart is anxious
To dance into
The edge of the horizon
Where the Angels
Soar - along
Whisper sweet nothings
More soothing
Than Hallelujah
More comforting
Than Leonard's Song

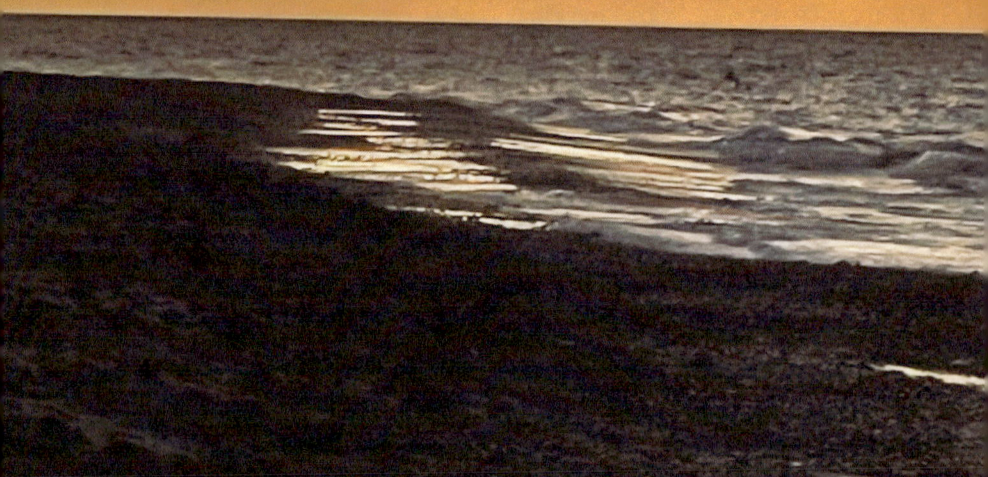

power of love

Off we stood
In the distance
Walking in the sand
Stood for
A moment
Holding
Hand in hand
We felt the beauty
We felt so alive
We know
What it feels like
We know
The Power
Of Love

feel the light

It's when
I wake
At midnight
Wrapped
In a Dream State
It's my
Time for reflection
Feeling a sigh - Of relief
Knowing - That we've made It
Been able
To find our way
Couldn't have done it
Without you
Without our Family
And Friends
And those
Silent Little Prayers
That flickered
Like a Candle
Glowing the Night
Opened our eyes
To Feel it
We've found
What we needed
We've found
Our Guiding Light

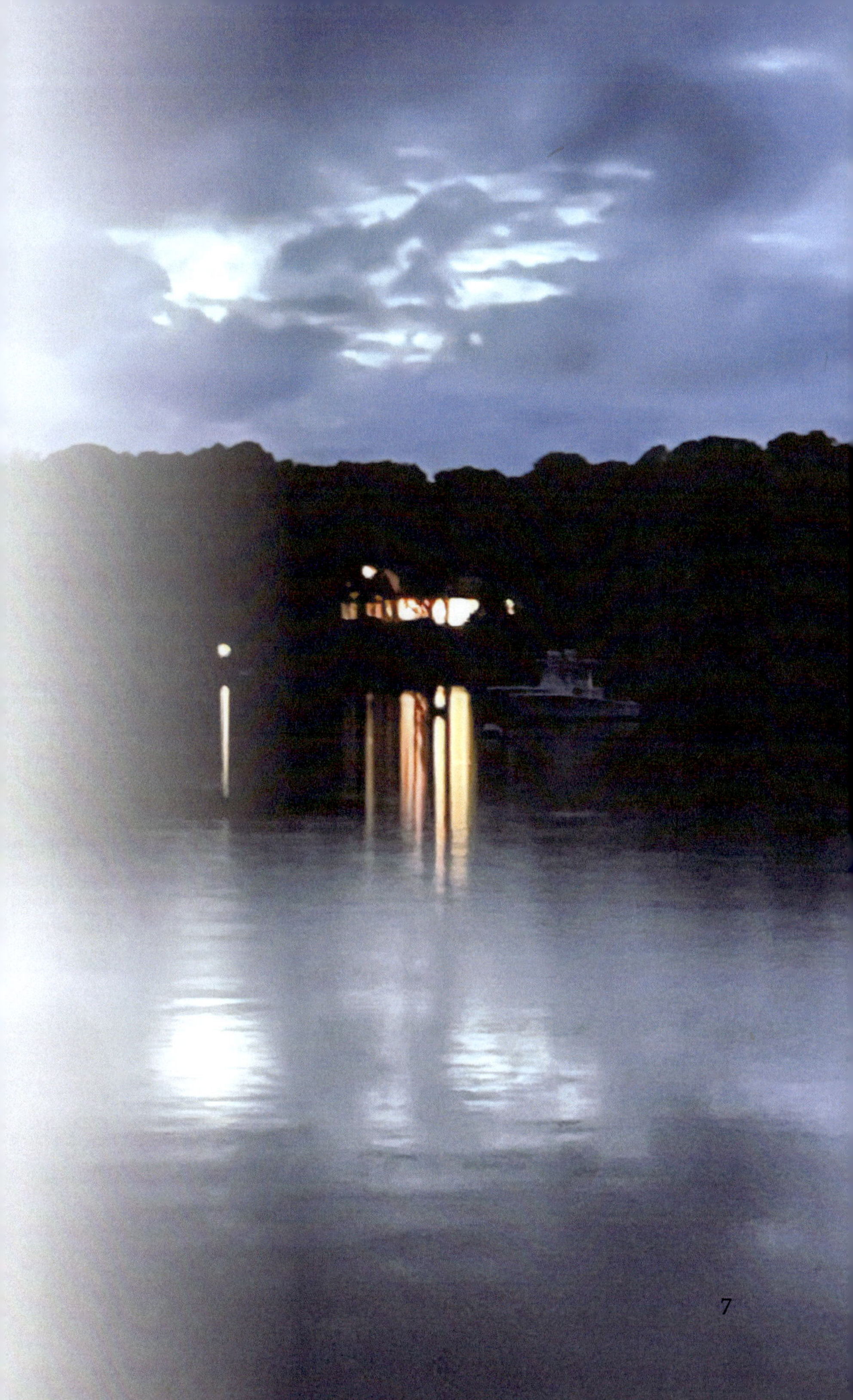

scent of silence

The breeze
Rushed across
Your face
Your hair
Played catch Up
When you rode your bike
To find the spot
You call - Your place
Where you can walk
Along a sandy shore
Saturated
With the sights
And - the sounds
Of the shades
And the colors
That sing
Your song
That Serenades
Your soul
With the sweetest
Scent of silence
Whispering
To the Horizon
As it welcomes
The entrance of Glory
The Silence
Of the Night

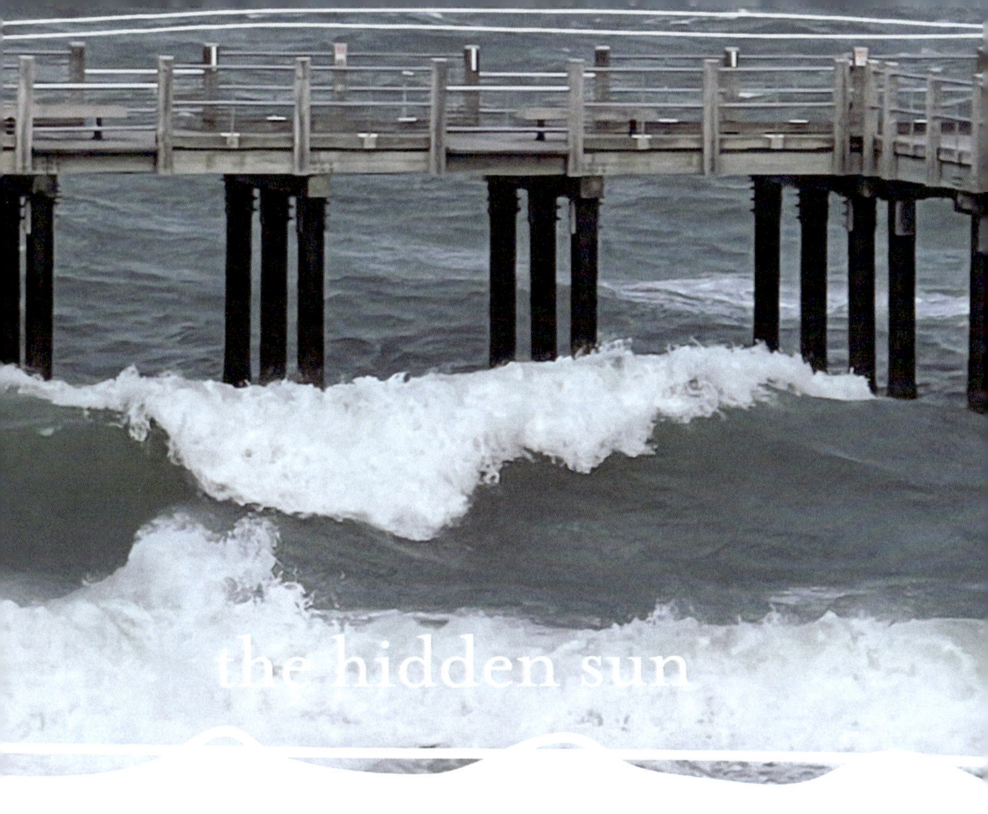

Winds took over
Sun hid behind
The cloud's
Rain drops
Pitter - Patter
Waves doing
Whatever they want
What's
On their mind
On this day
They remind us
Of their power
And their might

Storms moving
Up the coast
On into the night
People
They be fleeing
To more
Secure ground
Changing of
The Season
Rain didn't want to leave
Kept on Pounding
Just kept pounding
Through the night

the image

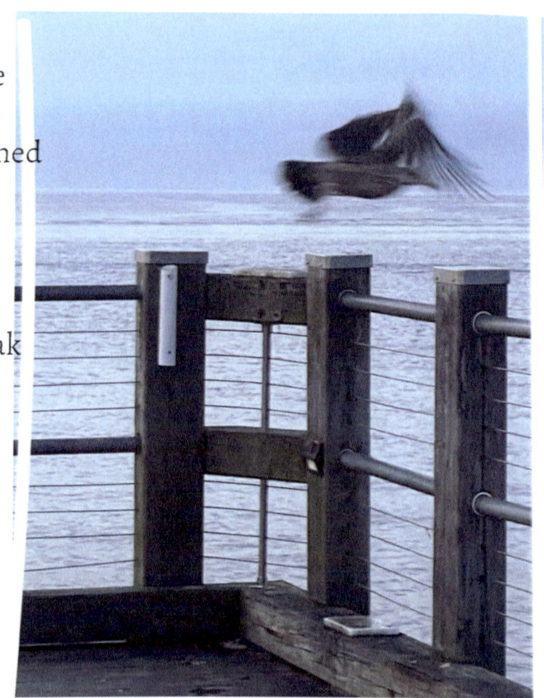

I saw an image
In the sky
Just a glimpse
Feathers fly
Walked to the edge
Of the pier
Stopped and Listened
God was near
I Looked
At the place
Inside my Heart
Didn't need to speak
Felt that spark
Stood in silence
Didn't need to
Say a Word
But I Knew
I'd find it
Because
I could
Feel It
Knew
I'd find it
Because - I heard

can't find the sun

Time caught me
Bound me up
Wrapped me - so tight
Just need a puff
Of Nature's fragrance
A Spray of Salty air
Walk along
The path
By the Pier
That sits between
The earth
And the ocean
Rippled waves
Splash on high
Birds - look in wonder

Fly on by
No perch
For feather
No bird pictures
No children jumping
No fishing lines dangling
Just a lot of nothing
Just a simple Pier
Sitting there
Doing nothing
Waiting
For the Sun
To break
While I'm
Standing by the Pier

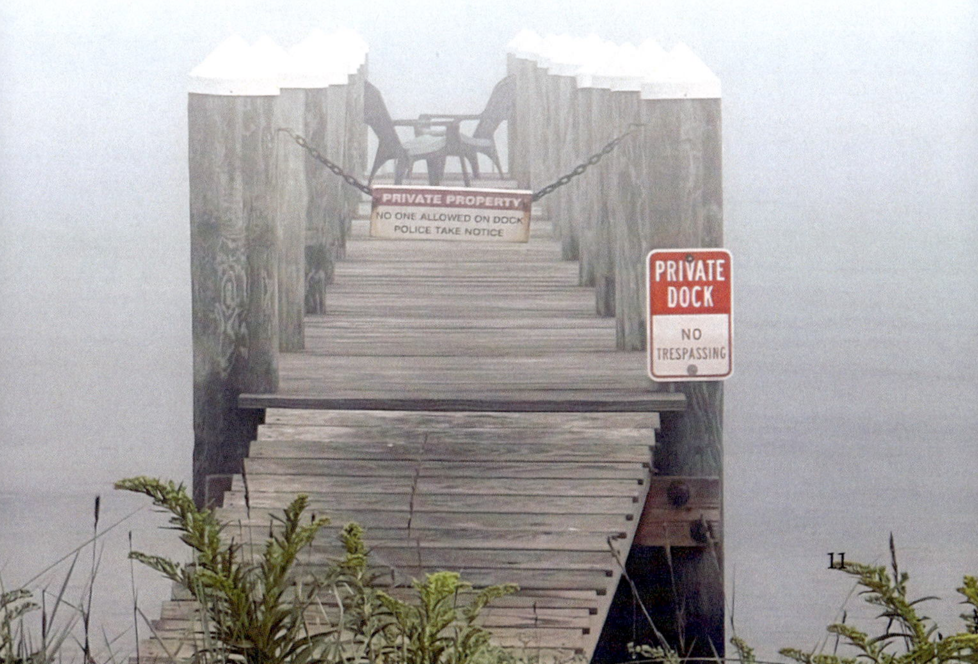

morning fog

I waited
By the Sea Shore
Watched morning's fog
Painted a picture
Not quite as clear
As a bell
If you look
Too deeply
It will draw you
Into the yonder
Cast you in a spell
Have you ever
Wondered what
It feels like
To walk - on a cloud
Floating on an image
Have you ever seen a
mirage
Listen for - fog horn's echo
Bouncing off
Changing shades of light
Hoping you will - do It
Entice You
To - Walk the stairway
Walk the flight
Draw you in
Like a moth
Help you
To do it
Help you
To find the light

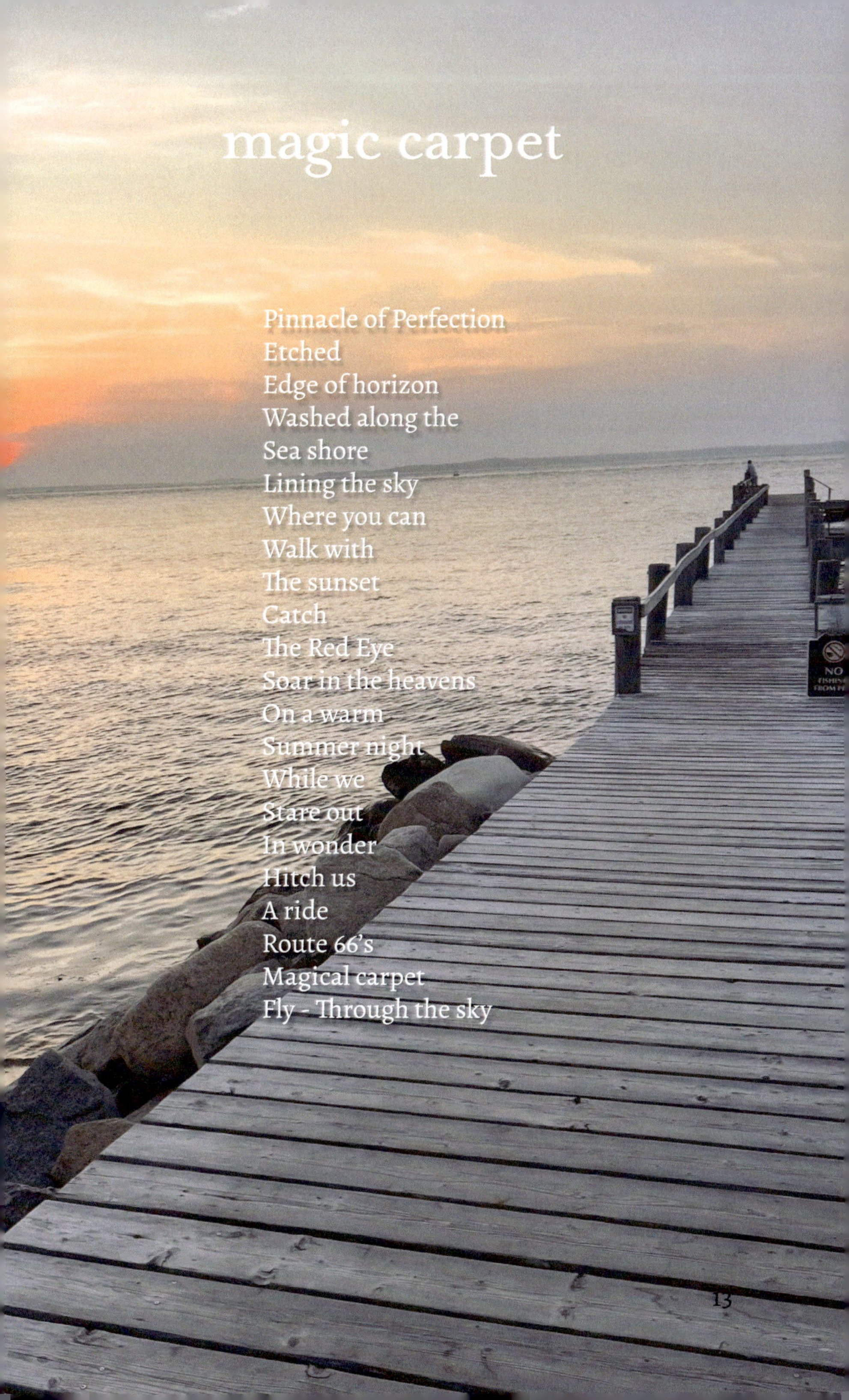

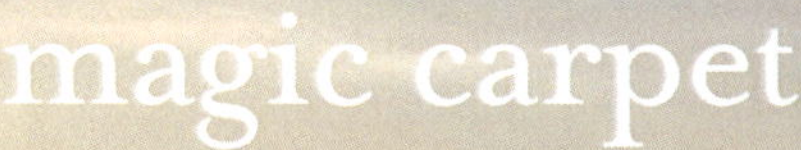

magic carpet

Pinnacle of Perfection
Etched
Edge of horizon
Washed along the
Sea shore
Lining the sky
Where you can
Walk with
The sunset
Catch
The Red Eye
Soar in the heavens
On a warm
Summer night
While we
Stare out
In wonder
Hitch us
A ride
Route 66's
Magical carpet
Fly - Through the sky

lazy days

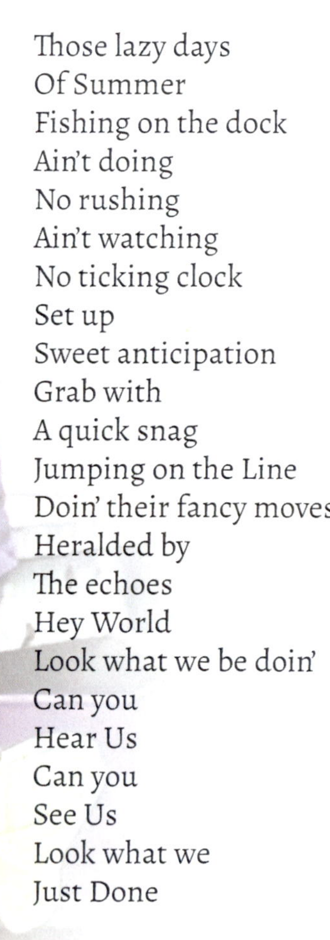

Those lazy days
Of Summer
Fishing on the dock
Ain't doing
No rushing
Ain't watching
No ticking clock
Set up
Sweet anticipation
Grab with
A quick snag
Jumping on the Line
Doin' their fancy moves
Heralded by
The echoes
Hey World
Look what we be doin'
Can you
Hear Us
Can you
See Us
Look what we
Just Done

he tried

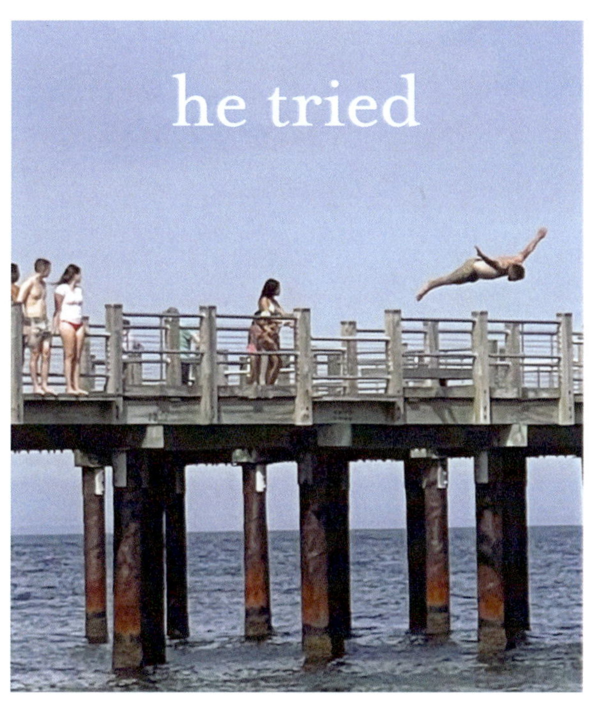

They told Him
He couldn't
Do It
No matter
How hard
He tried
Told him
The only ones
Can do It
Are the birds
Up in the sky
He asked
For just a moment

Spread wings
Like an angel
Much to
Their amazement
He proved
That he could do it
Took
That leap of faith
Soared through the air
Proved to the world
He could do it
He did it
He tried

amazing grace

I swear
She winked
At me
In the shadows
Looked at me
Through the fog
Looked me in the eye
Said good morning
Put on
Her biggest smile
Said she remembered
Last time we met
Had our little chats
Even sent me
An invitation
To join her
And her mighty crew
Who slip through
The ocean
Move against the tides
Waves started cheering
Kissing of the bow
Oars synchronizing

To the beat
Of the heart
Of the morning
Pulse racing
To pitch fever
As she sailed
Into the sunset
Tears welled
In the echoes
I have to leave
I gotta go
I'll say farewell
For the moment
It's not our time
To Say - Goodbye

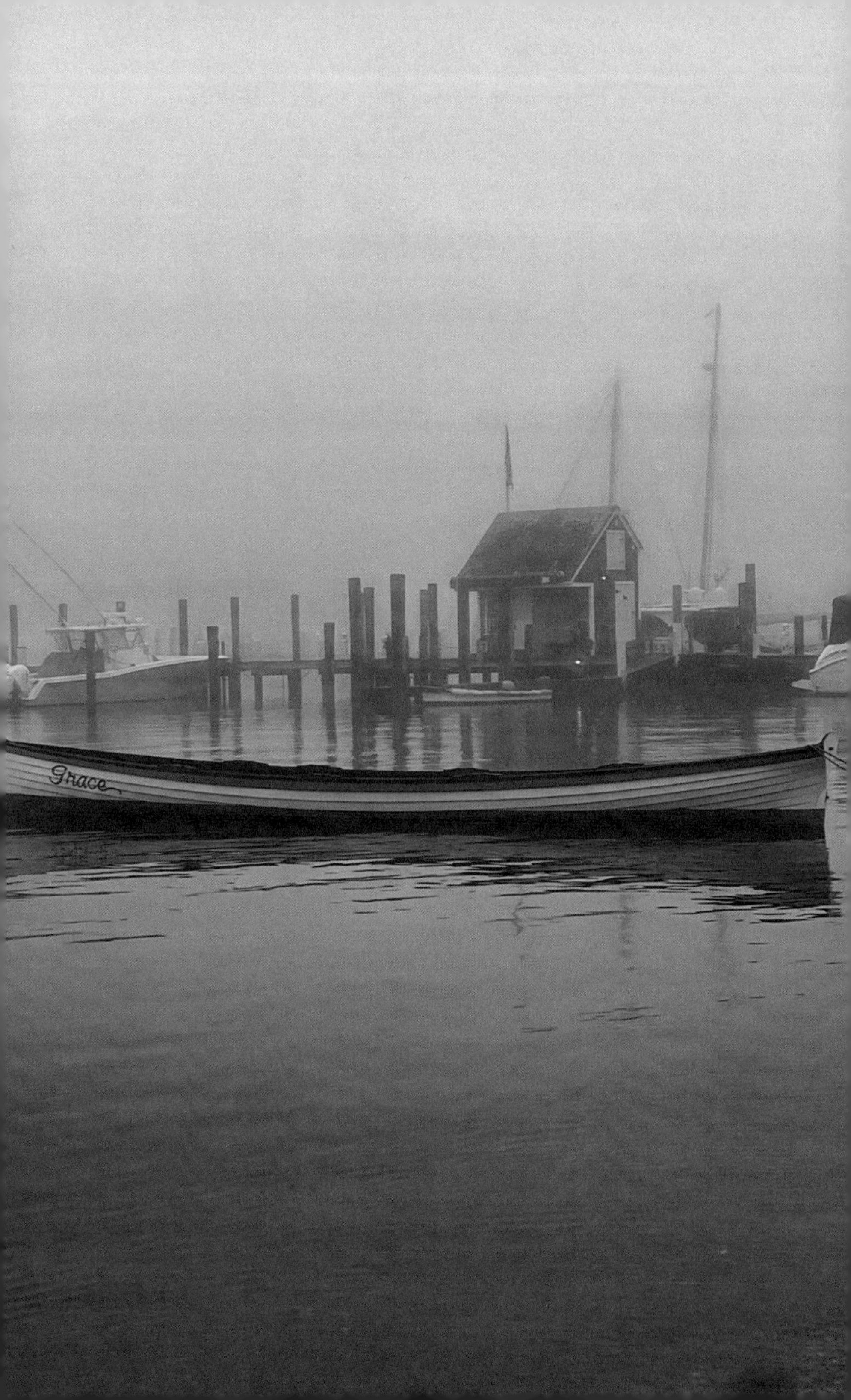
Grace

jar of hope

Silver streaks
Of pixie dust
Skim along
The waters
Spread across the Seas
Wondered
What would happen
If I took my jar of hope
Sprinkle it into the
The depths
Of the Ocean
Let it flow with ease
Will it make a difference
Will it bring a smile
To an elder's face
Would it help the young
Trying to find their destiny
Trying to find their place
In history
Just a single ripple
Just a single drop
In the depths
That reverberates
Like thunder
Of an incoming storm
Will it bring
Peace and Harmony
Will it make it
Through - The Storm

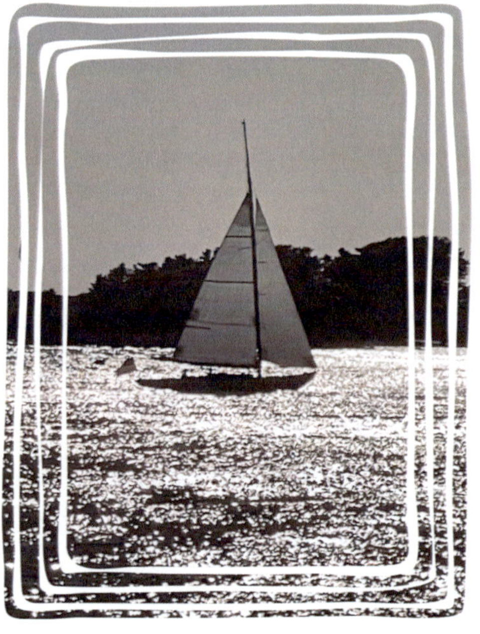

follow your wonder

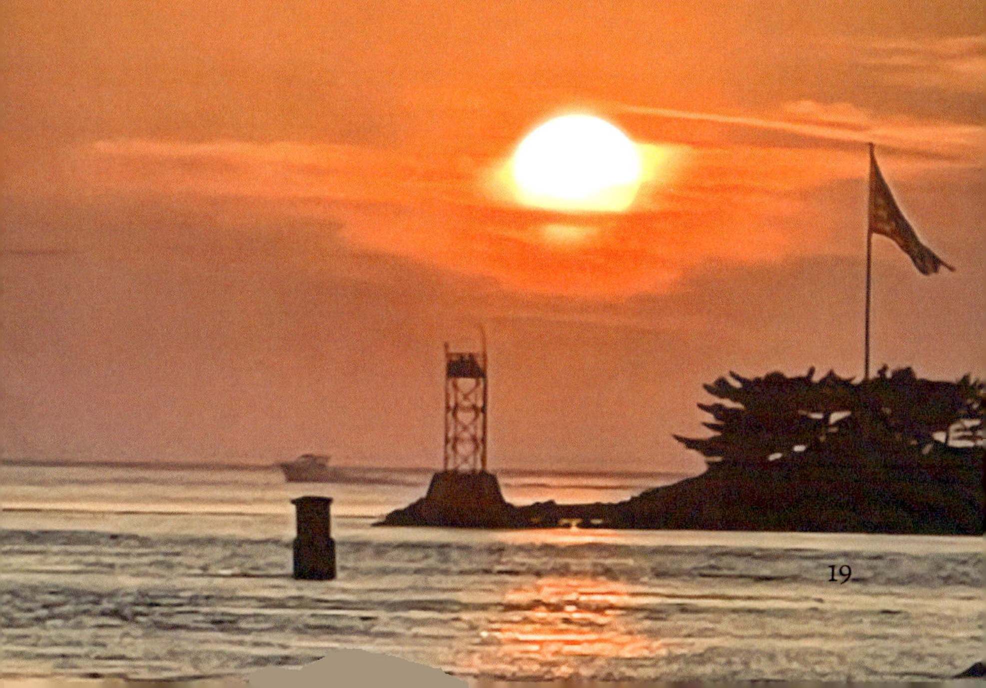

Follow your passion
Till the Sun
Fades - Into the Ocean
Follow your Wonder
Until the day
You die
Let nothing
Come between us
Let - nothing
Take the winds
From The flames
Of desire
'Cause - you can't leave

No footsteps
In the Ocean
But - you can
Walk - to the stars
The - long flight
Find your Happy Place
in Paradise
On the
Edge Of the Universe
On The Island
That warms your heart
Through those
Cold - Winter Nights

book of love

Summertime
Has left me
Flew into night's sky
She wandered
Into the sunset
Preparing
For a long
Sweet Lullaby
Where we
Dream - In harmony
Walk the beach
Holding hands
Like Young lovers
Do the - tango
To the - rhythm
To the - beat

Of a Spanish Latin Band
Who embraced
For the moment
Do the do
Do the dance
Of Night's Adventure
Until the Sun
Calls for Spring
To rise the tides
Wash the sand
Of our footprints
Fresh start
To a new path
A new chapter
In - The Book Of Love

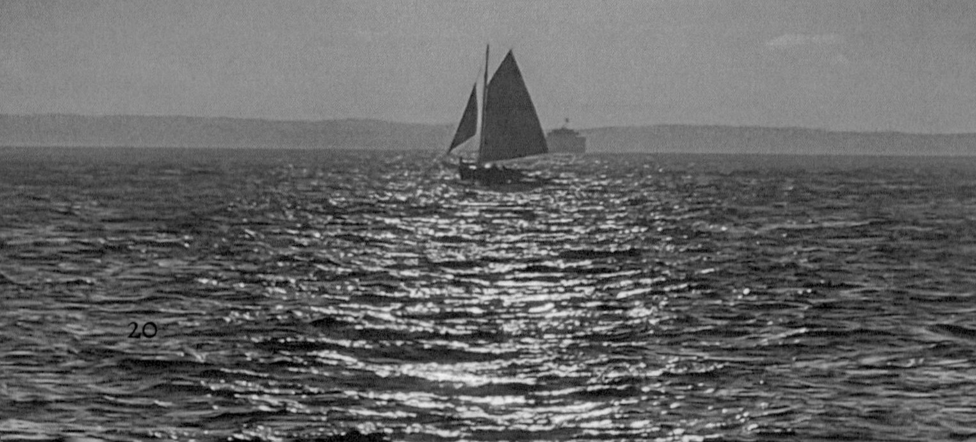

edge of time

Her silence
Talks to me
To my heart
To my soul
Each day
Flies by
Leaving a trail
Of messages
To behold
I've tried listening
In the city
Amidst rolling tires
And beeping horns
Can best
Be tuned in
If you look
From a place
Where your
Eyes can stretch
Your Imagination
On a clear day
With a clear view
Of the horizon
Unobstructed by anything
Except - The edge of time
Flying by

hitting the stride

Do you remember
That Summer
Do you remember
The Day
We spent
On the beach
At Oak Bluffs
So much
Going on
People - walking
People - talking
People - sitting
On sandy beach chairs

Kids playing
Like song birds
Singing their songs
Romping - in Ocean waters
Splashing all around
We were having
Such a good time
Having a ball
We never wanted to
Leave there
Never wanted
That - day to end

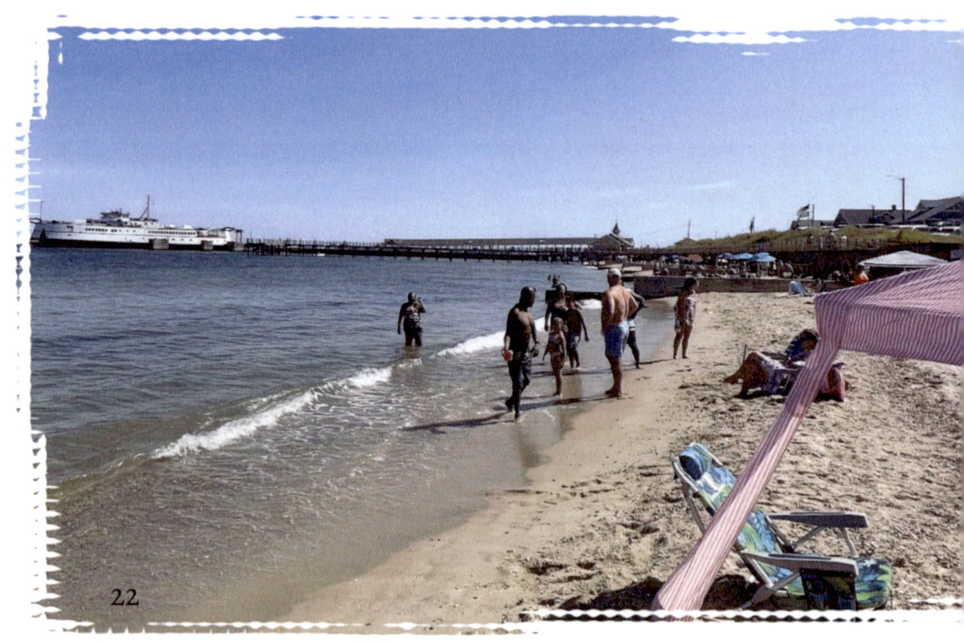

tied in knots

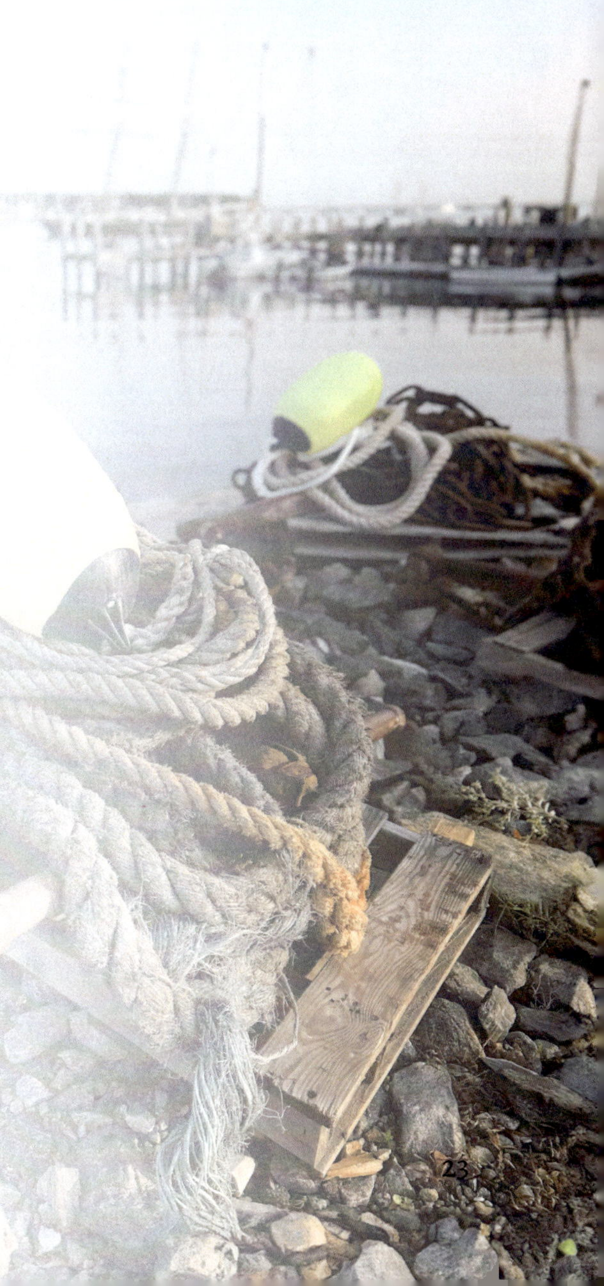

Amidst
Morning's silence
When things
Could easily
Get tied in knots
I listen with patience
Lickety - tick
Of the clock
Wave the hand
Come Hither
Old Friend - Of mine
Take a seat
For the moment
Listen to the Scent
Of the Breeze
Until our Hearts
Feel the Music
Falling of the leaves
Sit and Stare
For hours
Engage - In idle chatter
Waves - Pitter Patter
Changing
Of the Tide

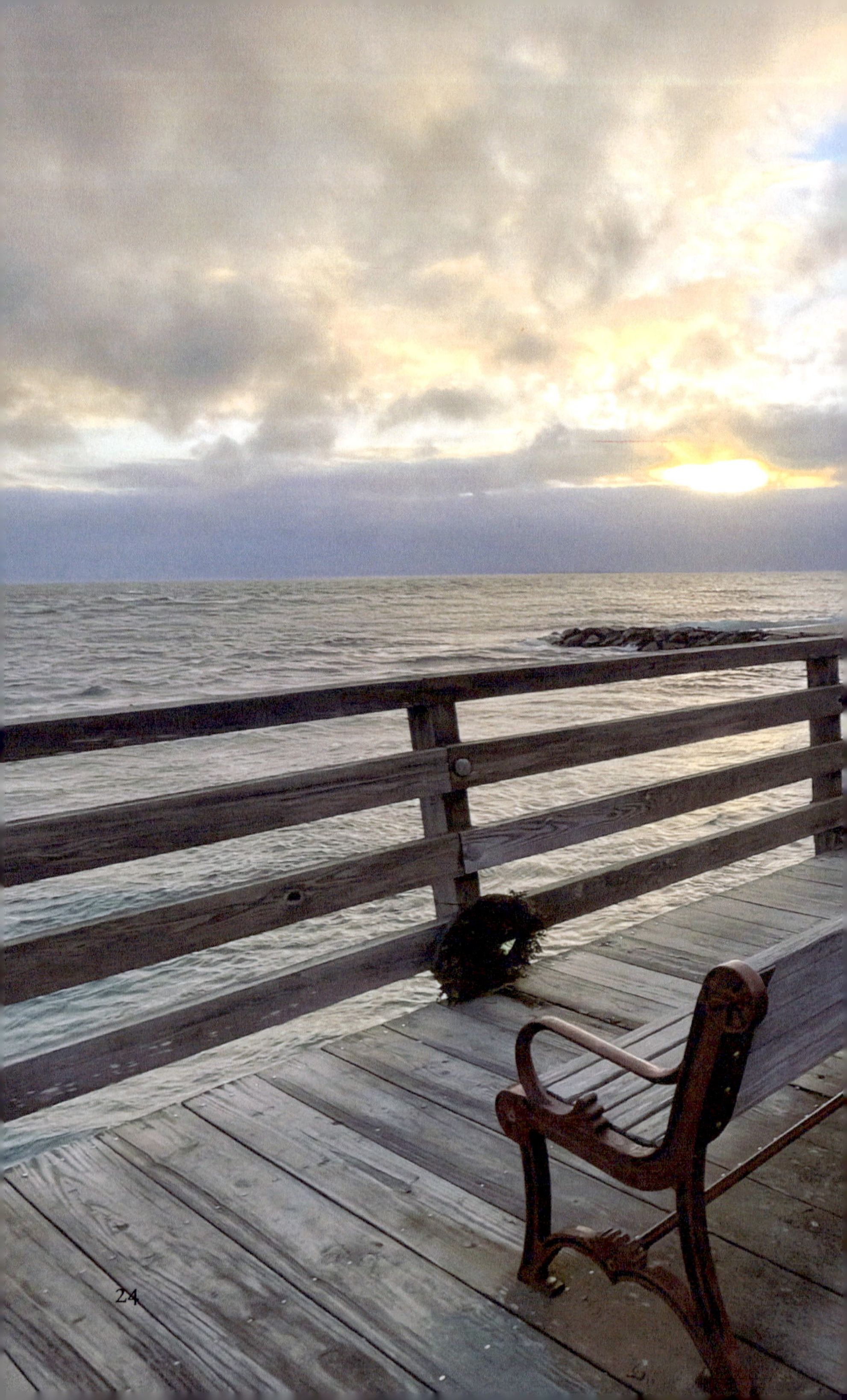

there no more

Morning's silence
Walked towards me
Looked me
In the eye
I asked
If she could
Hear the silence
Her lips glistened
As I whispered
Ever so softly
You are so beautiful
You are my morning light
You make my heart pound
You helped me
Feel the life
I kept walking
Didn't hear no footsteps
Didn't hear the sound
All of a sudden
Out of nowhere
There was an
Angelical silence
That grabbed my attention
Opened curiosity's door
Turned around abruptly
Eyes looking afar
Mysteriously vanished
Was there no more

south beach stream

I couldn't help
But notice
The meandering
Of the stream
Winding towards
Sun's reflection
Delicacy of sweet dreams
That I've haphazardly
Entered
Following the path
On the road
To happiness
Can't find on no map

Don't never
Want to
Leave it
Don't want
To lose
My pace
I'm gonna roll
Down that Highway
Think I've found it
Gonna claim it
Gonna name it
My Happy Place

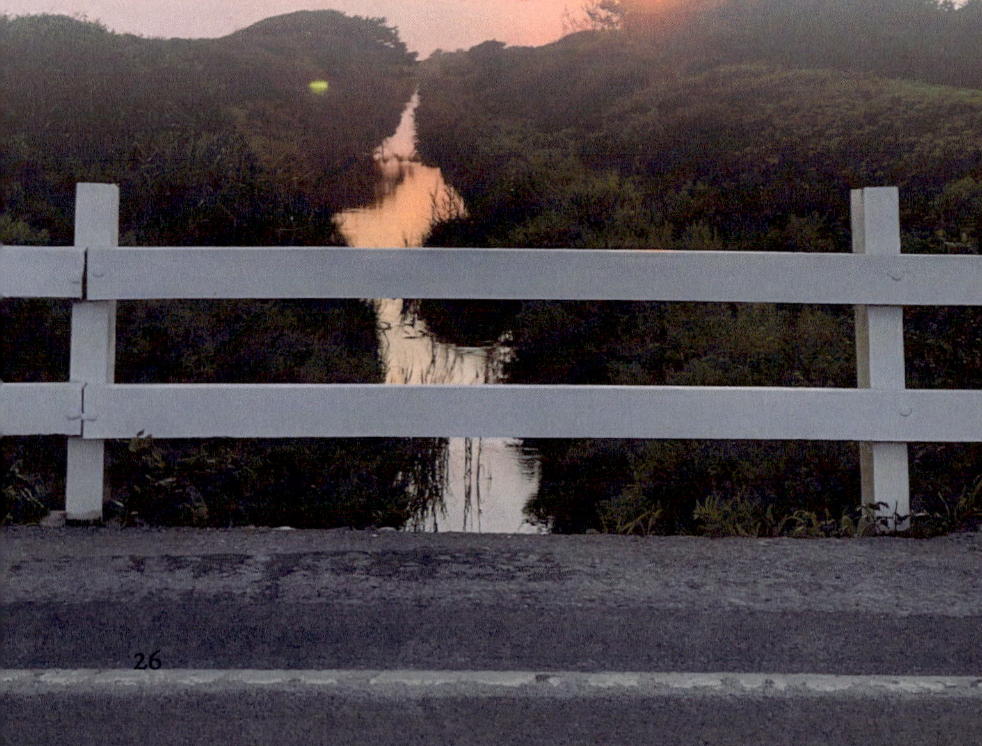

edgartown lighthouse

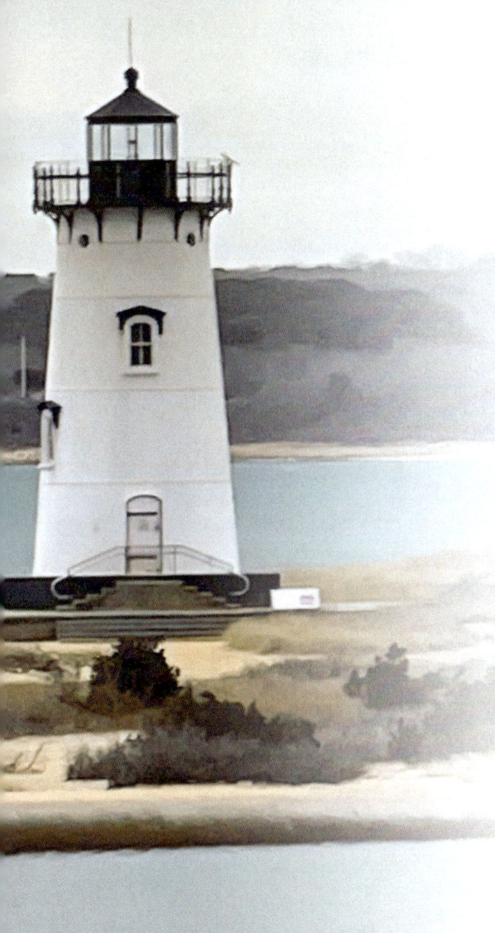

She's seen 'em
Weathered the storms
She's standing there
Humming her song
Wedding party
Gathered around
Boats of Summer
Sailing the Sound
She's one of those people
Brings out the best
Still hanging around
Stood the test
No matter how things
change
She stays the same
Old Style Lady
She knows how to
Play the Game

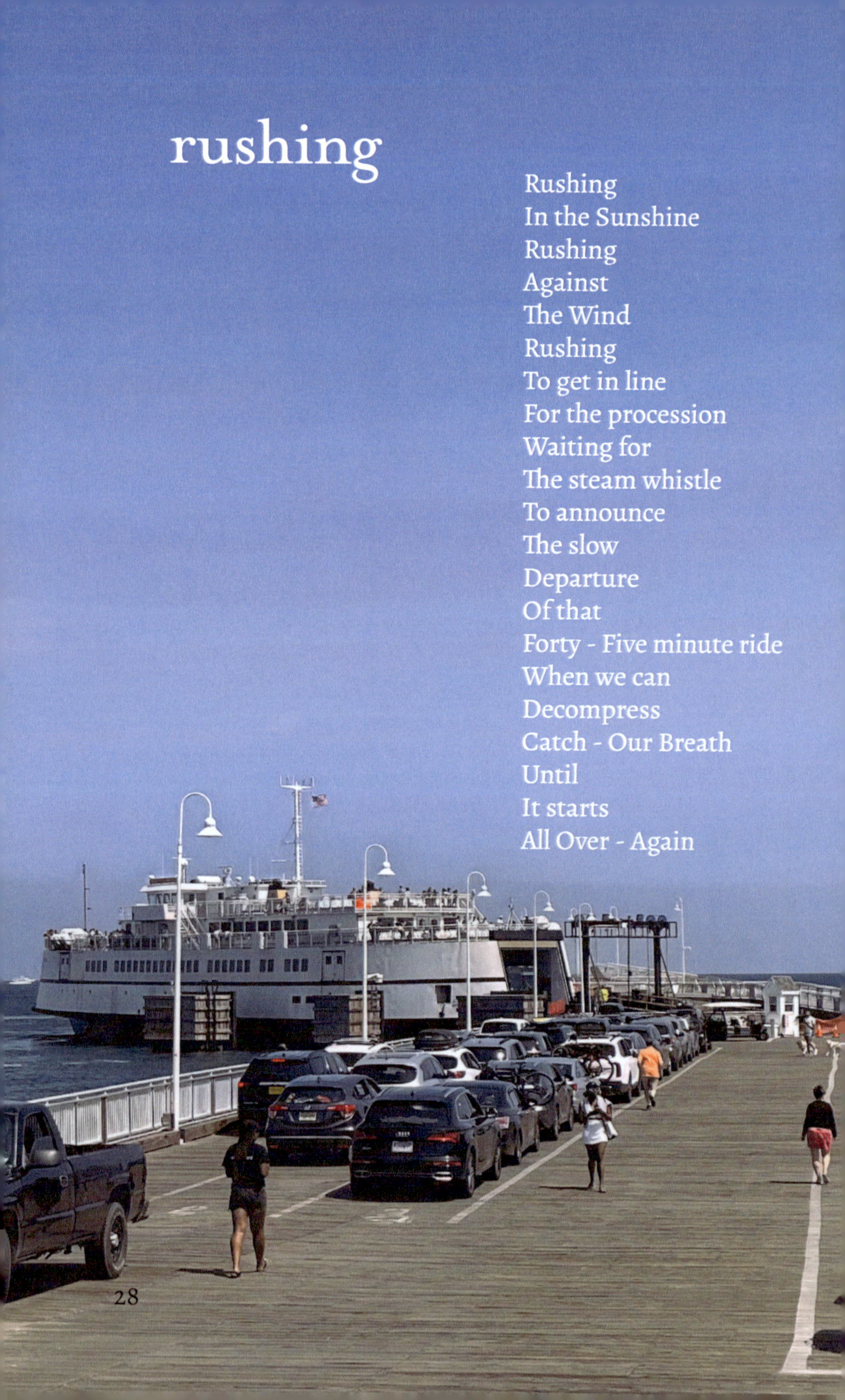

rushing

Rushing
In the Sunshine
Rushing
Against
The Wind
Rushing
To get in line
For the procession
Waiting for
The steam whistle
To announce
The slow
Departure
Of that
Forty - Five minute ride
When we can
Decompress
Catch - Our Breath
Until
It starts
All Over - Again

the shuttle

We sat for hours and hours
Overlooking the shuttle
Watching the changing - Of the guard
Follow the ferry boats
Float 'em in
Pack 'em up
Get 'em off
Cars with those Thules
Bike rack on the back
Kids and the pet dog
Hanging out the windows
As the car rolls
Down the gangplank
Greeted by a Drum Roll
Rumbling planks
Marking the gateway
To adventures - To fantasies - To fun
Where everyone leaves
Heartaches and worries
On the other side of the shore
Once your feet hit - The Island
Kick your feet up high
Time to lay back
Set your Clock to Island Time
Where everything's
Slow and easy
No rushing - No fussing - No muss
Don't never - Want to Leave
Don't Never - Want to - Go Back

simple things

It's restorative
Chock full
Everything - that's Natural
Everything's - Infused
With Sunshine's
Mist that lingers
Across the horizon
Spread across - the Sea
Where you can go - On a spree
Spending the most
Valuable of what you've worked for
Just to indulge in simple things
Like splashing the water
Dancing in the rain
Hovering with the Seagulls
Never searching in vain
Where you can feast
Upon those
Tasty treats
Just a pinch of - Windswept Sand
Sprinkled upon
Sea Side Sandwiches
Where you graze
While you gaze
Where you can
Do what you've always wanted
Stop time - Throw the Clock Into the water
Sink to the Bottom of the Sea
To let this day
Last for forever
Buzz around - Like a Bee

join me at the inkwell

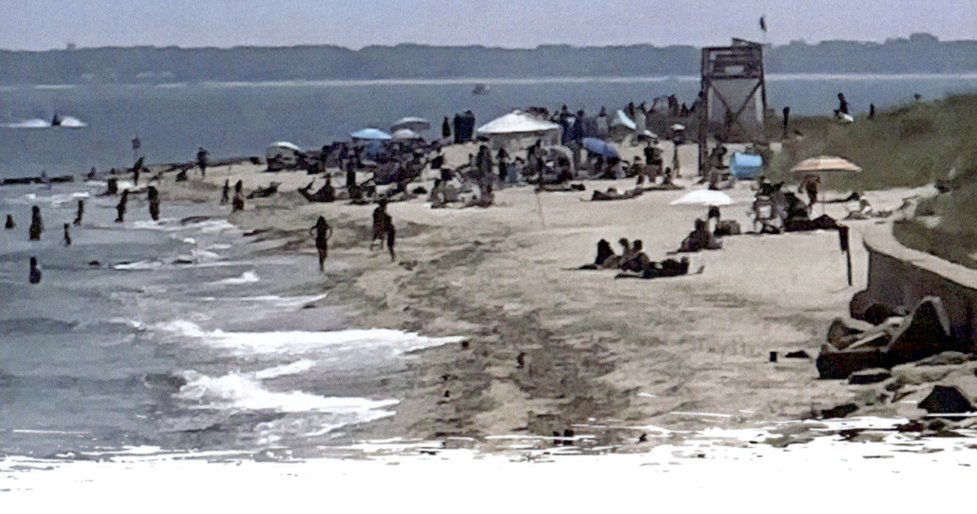

Waves Brushed
Winds Blew
Whispers
Into the air
Calling out
To one and all
Come join in
All the fun
A place
Where - Children Gather
Build Sand Castles
In the sky
A place - To sit in Wonder
Under
A warm
Summer Sky

attention seekers

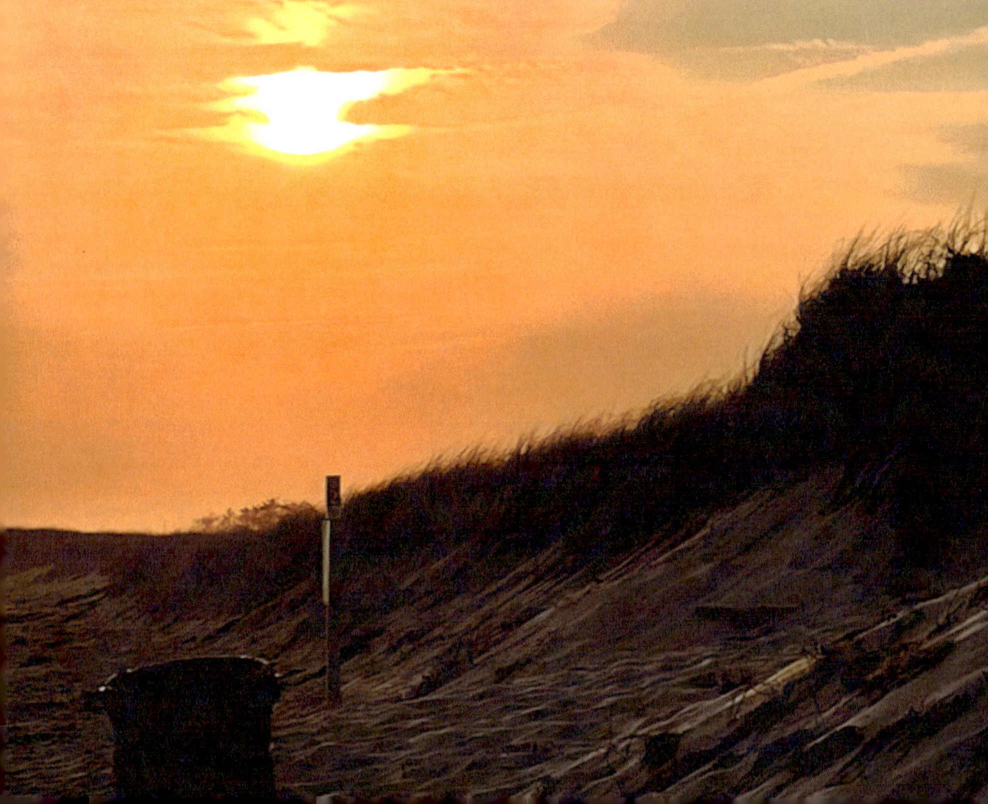

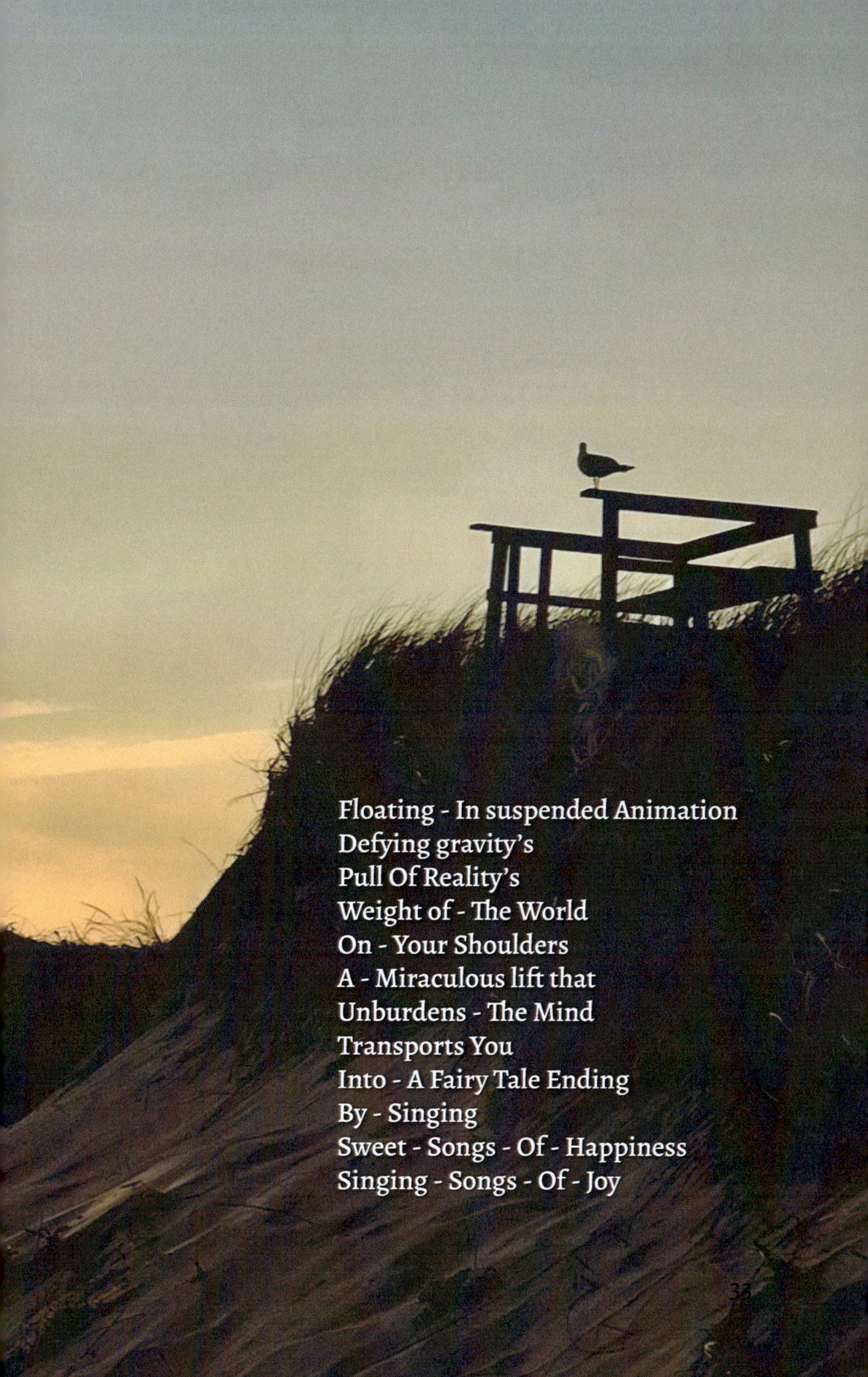

Floating - In suspended Animation
Defying gravity's
Pull Of Reality's
Weight of - The World
On - Your Shoulders
A - Miraculous lift that
Unburdens - The Mind
Transports You
Into - A Fairy Tale Ending
By - Singing
Sweet - Songs - Of - Happiness
Singing - Songs - Of - Joy

33

for a midsummer's night dream

An Island
Looked me in the Eyes
Was I Dreaming
My Heart couldn't
Tell the difference
My feet couldn't
Feel the ground
They were - Walking on a Rainbow
They were - Floating on a Cloud
Then - She reached
Her arms so gently
She hugged me
She set my Heart on fire
That floated
Into - Nocturnal's Silence
Danced into
The - Evening's Sky
Fell asleep - Slumbered
Into - My Heart's Desire

feeling - island's life

Waking Light
Asked the Question
Was I Dreaming
Cause my Heart
Is still Racing
Trying to
Catch my Breath
That Was - Stolen
By an Island's Interlude
During - A brief
A Cherished moment
On a warm
And - Memorable
Island's Summer Night
That was filled
With bursts
Of Delicate Flowers
That filled the
Night with
Showers of Fireworks
Bursting - Glowing light
That was followed
By the thunder
Of bursting Stars
That filled - my heart

That filled - the Sky
With - The flutter
Felt like an - Earth Quake
Shook - The Ground - So hard
Filled my Eyes
With Tears
Like it was
The Fourth of July

purge your troubles

A Day at the Beach
Is a lot more
Simple than it seems
We all cherish
Those moments
To bask in the Sun
To dip our toes
In the Ocean
To listen to the wind
As it blows
Our mind away
From the Daily Drudge
To Purge all
Our Troubles Away
Eat a Piece of Fudge
Along the Boulevard
Where - Merry Goes Around
Children reaching - For - Brass Rings
Just dropped
Their - Slice of Pizza
On the Ground
Where footsteps
Walk - with excitement
To - The West Side
AKA - The Chop

Where all eyes
Peer out
To Watch - The Sunset
As it - Slowly
Slowly Drops
Into - The Sound

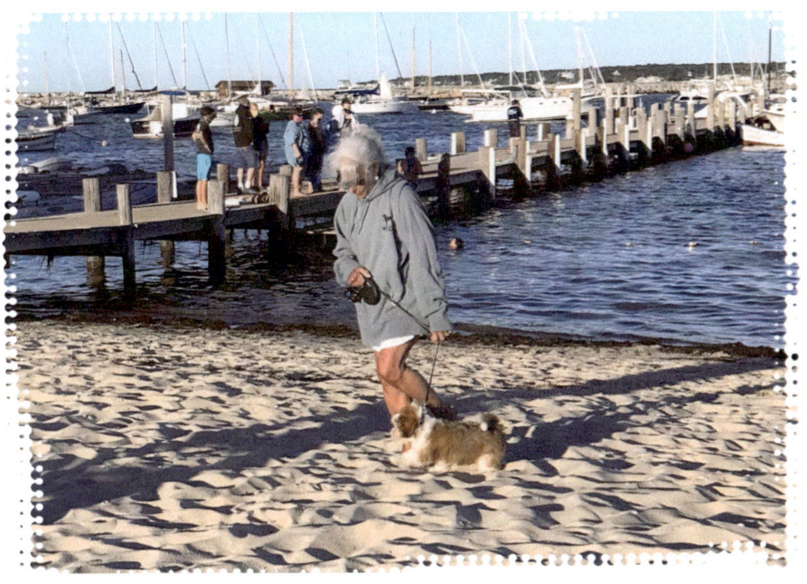

the jetty

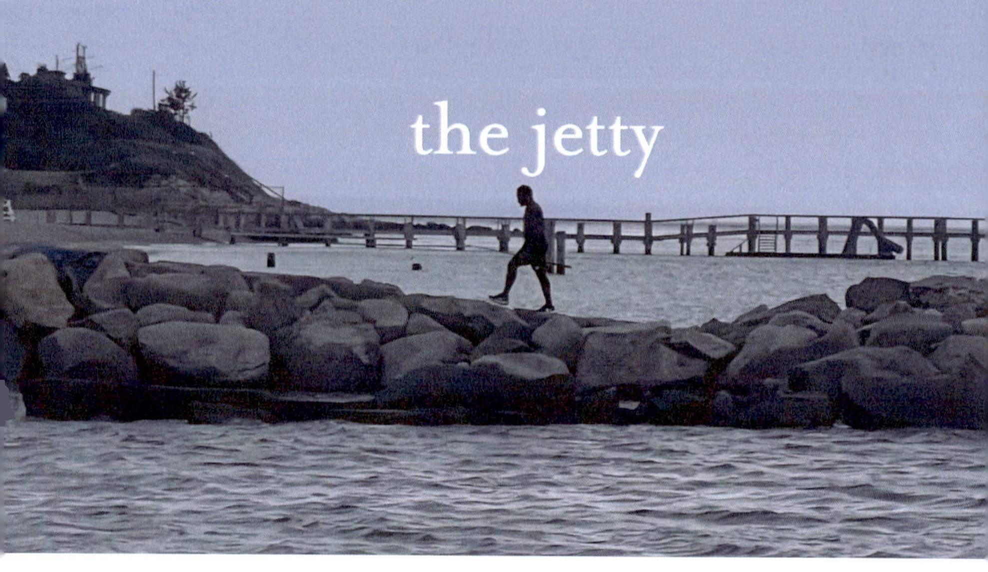

Walk Ocean's Water
Walk along the Sea
Where silence
Speaks louder
Than anyone
Can - See
Or - Feel
What is needed
What we - Crave Inside
To listen
To the - Rhythm
Of the Ocean
To feel the
Turning - Tide
That warms us
In the evening
From our heads
To our toes
That Skip
Along the Jetty
More Soothing
Than - A Story of Old

speck of sand

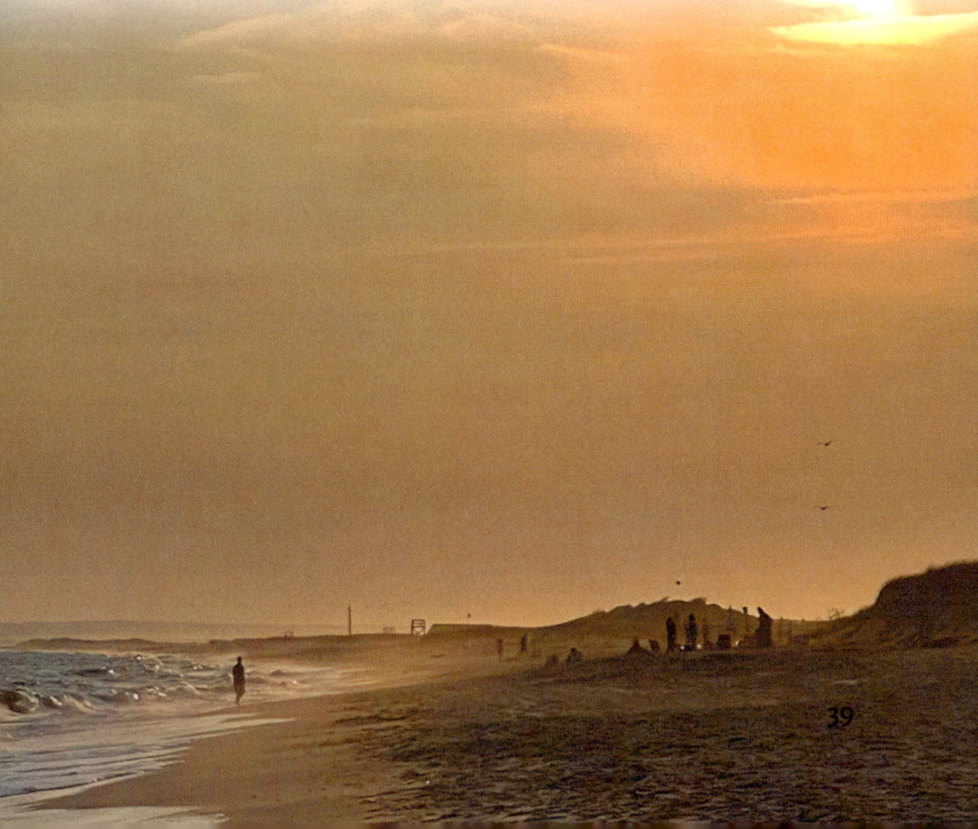

In the relative
Scheme of things
We are but a drop
In the Ocean
A mere speck
In the sand
That fades into
The Evening
That greets
The rolling tide
We have but

A brief moment
To proclaim
Our - Mission
Our - Purpose
Our - Worth
By planting our footprints
Into the sands - Of time
Only to have them
Washed away
By the flow
Of morning's tide

a - lot - about - nothing

Nothing - Nothing
Absolutely - Nothing
Can come close
Can come near
To the feeling - That I get
When I sit by the Ocean
At Sunset
Mesmerized - By the Waves
By the rhythm
By their sound
That washes my Worries
Into - Ocean Waters
Open the door - Of Tranquility
To Find - The right fabric
To weave a - Magic carpet
Guaranteed - Peace of Mind
Designed to Comfort
Designed to Soothe
Those - Aches
Those - Pains
Of the - Daily Grind
Don't need
No - Beach Chair to sit on
Don't mind
That little bit
Of sand in my pockets
Cause - it's Good
For - The Heart
And - So Good
For - The Soul

moon drops

As Tranquil
And - As Silent
As Moon-drops
Dripping
Into the Sea
Where Mermaids
Wait - with the Patience
Of an Angel
So no one else
Can See
Where they go at Sunset
Dancing along the Shore
Keep searching
For the secret
To open up the door
To your imagination
Let your vision
Run wild
Run free
Run like - Untamed Horses
As free
As free
Can be

tomorrow's day

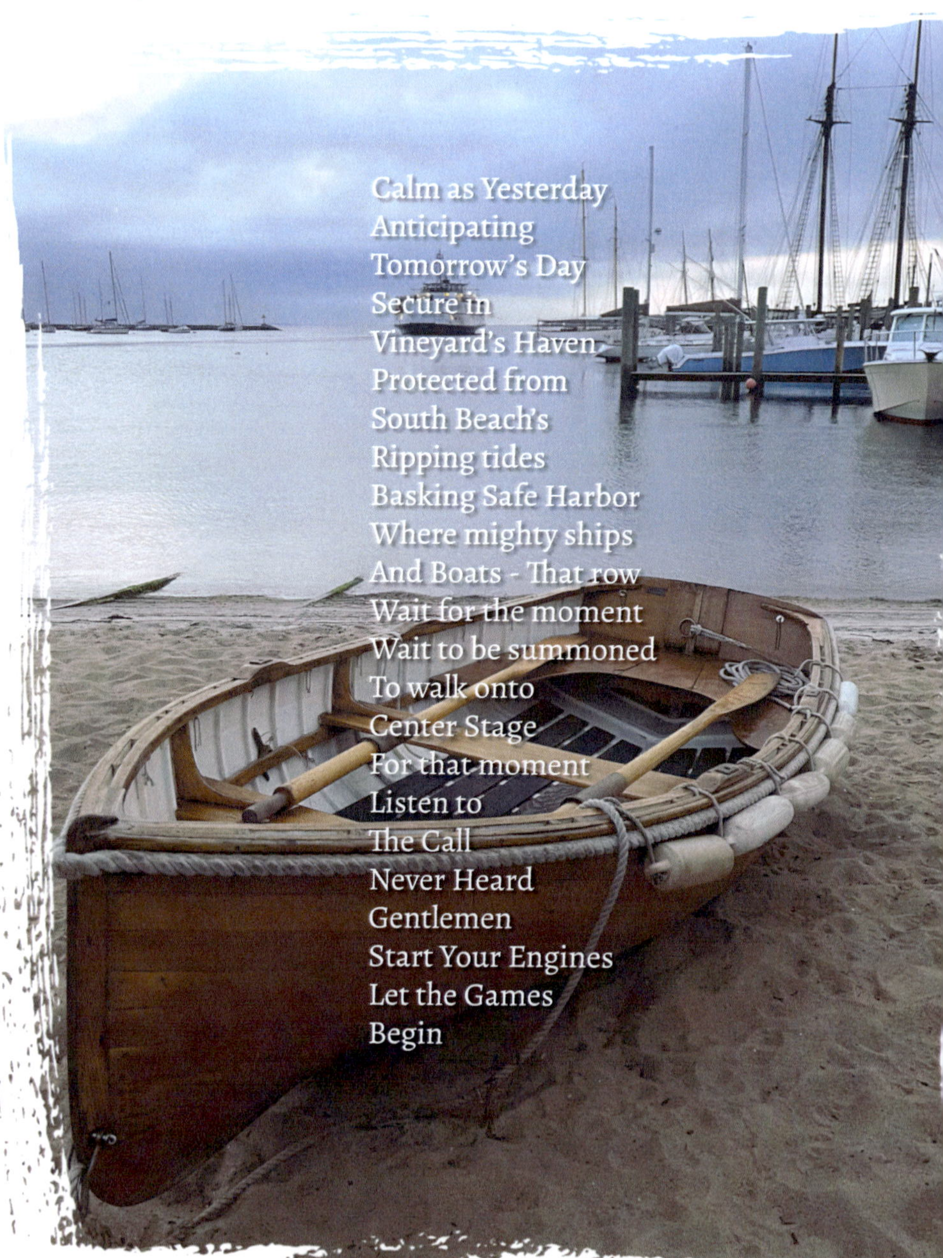

island life

Island Life - Filled with Spice
Bare feet - Sandy floor
Wake in the morning
Watch the Sun Rise
Spend the day at the Beach
Get there early
Before all the parking spaces
Dry up faster
Than blink - of an eye
Get together - For an evening meal
Do people really eat
Snails or Fried Eel
Lobster Ice Cream
Along Circuit Ave
Why is it
There are long lines
In a parking lot
That winds
To a - Back Door
Whose scent - Draws you in
Like moths - to light
Can't ask
For - Anything More
Kick up your heels
Let's all get together
Let's - Lite up - The Night

the excitement

Catch Excitement
Embrace the Thrill
Of dipping your toes into the chill
Of the Ocean
On a Hot Summer's Day
Or to take the plunge
From the bridge
Or the pier
Where your audience is captivated
By your Courage - Your dare
Maybe it's the
Quest to break
The World Record
For the number
Of brass rings
Nimble fingers
Can Fetch
With the speed - Of a Flying Horse
Compared only
To the skill
Of that brazing Seagull
Who had the Audacity
Who had the Nerve
To zoom in
Grab the Sandwich
Right out of your hands
Looked down - With laughter
Flew off - Into the sky

break from the heat

A day - on The Island
A day - at the Beach
One like no other
Break from the heat
Slip on Sandals
Dip your weary Feet
Ocean's waters
Gotta Love it
Can't be beat
Follow the Rhythm
Of Morning's glow
Chiming - with waves
On a mission
Gotta go
Wander the Dunes
Till the Sun reaches peak
Stops at Humphrey's
Vegetarian sandwich
Without the meat
When the Sun's
Getting ready
To call it a day
Load up at Menemsha's
Summer Snack
On the tray
Where you can
Pop the chilled bottle
Listen to the Fizz
As the Sun does its magic
Quick - As a Whiz

seeking adventure

I walked through
The Valley
Climbed the Mountains
Sailed the Ocean
Flew the Sky Blue
No matter
How far I Travel
New paths to find
Everything boils down
To one thing
This world
All its adventures
Are Yours for the taking
All you gotta do
Is to wake to the morning
Take - a deep breath
Take - that chance
Take - the first step
Open Your eyes
Look to the Sky
Whatever You want
Whatever Your needs
It's gonna be Yours
But You won't get it
If you don't take that chance
If you don't - Give it a try

seeking fame

Sunset's
Silhouette
Shadows
Standing
Sea's Sound
Begging
The question
Can you - see me
Can you - see me now
Spent a whole day's patience
Waiting - to be found
Tripod and canvas
Stroke - of the brush
With a little bit of luck
Will become as Famous
As - Mona Lisa
And - Her Smile

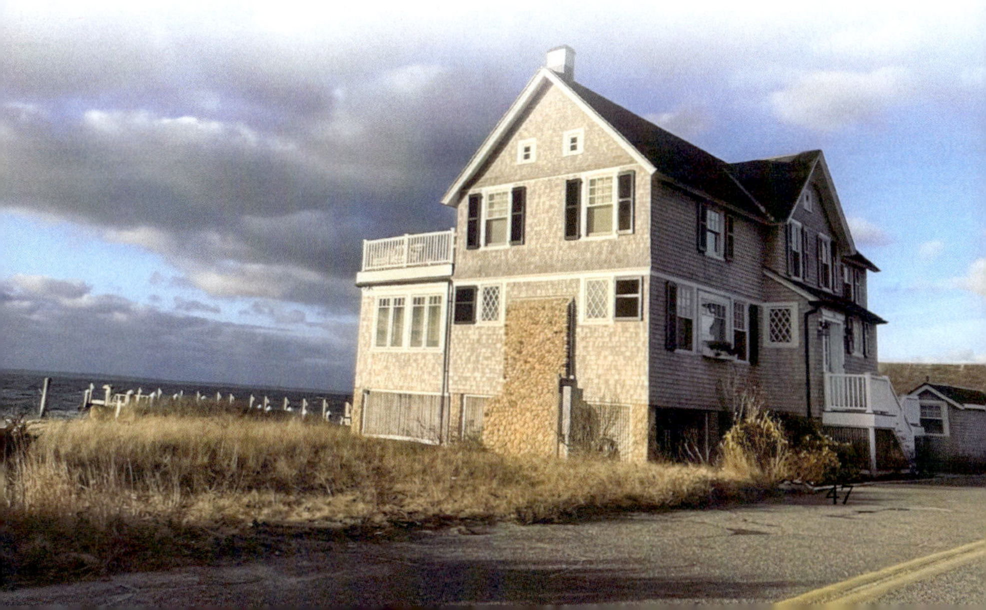

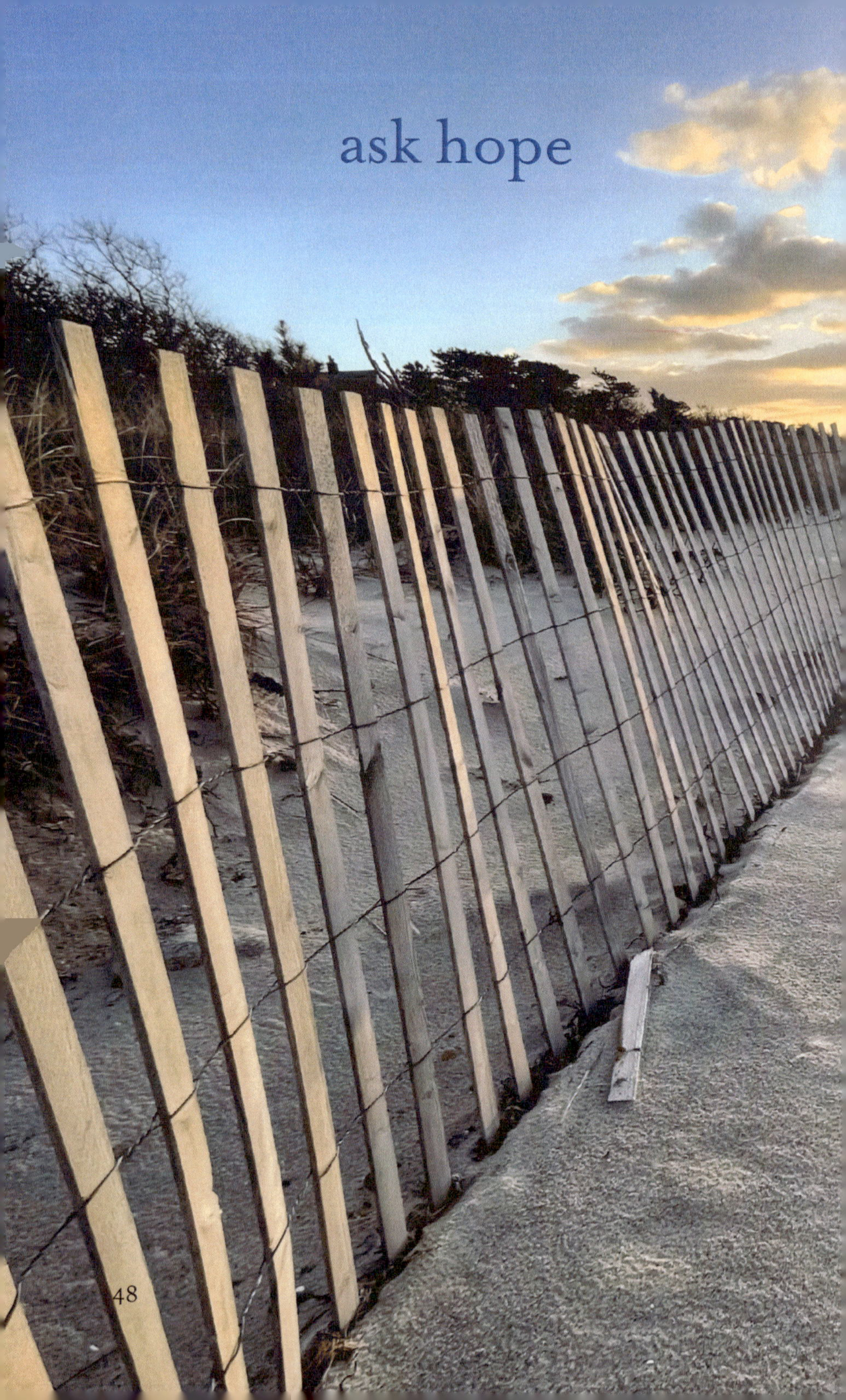
ask hope

Stretch your Arms
By your side
Open your Palms
To the sky
Tilt your Head
Look up High
Inhale
Until you feel
Breath's radiance
Wash the tears
Wash the fears
That weigh heavy
No matter
What happens
To you
No matter
What comes your way
You'll find
Peace Everlasting
If you ask Hope
To join you
Ask Hope
Be your Guide
Find the Faith
That will lead You
To the answer
Of your prayer
It's written in the Sky

innocence's essence

Sail - the Wind
Stroll - the Shore
Seize - the Moment
Catch your Breath
Respect - Our Mother
Place your shoes
Heaven's doorstep
Raindrops - Echo
Sweet Lyrics
Sweet essence of Innocence
Chalice - overflowing
Stand in for - Sunshine's - Absence
Embrace Life's
Simplest Pleasure
Before the Sun Sets
Seize the moment
Retreat - Rejoice
Refresh - Renew
Bow your Head
Silence - Anointed
Sing - Hallelujah
Sing - Celebration
Sing - To the Ocean
Celebrate - The New

promise of the land

Amidst - Chaos and
Confusion
Mixed with
Turmoil's froth
Found a Place
Where - Solitude
Wrapped in Silence
Leads us by the hand
That guides Us
Breaks through - The fog
To the promise
Of the land
Where those
Who tread - Before us
Walked the Pier
Jumped Aboard
Sailed - The Great Beyond

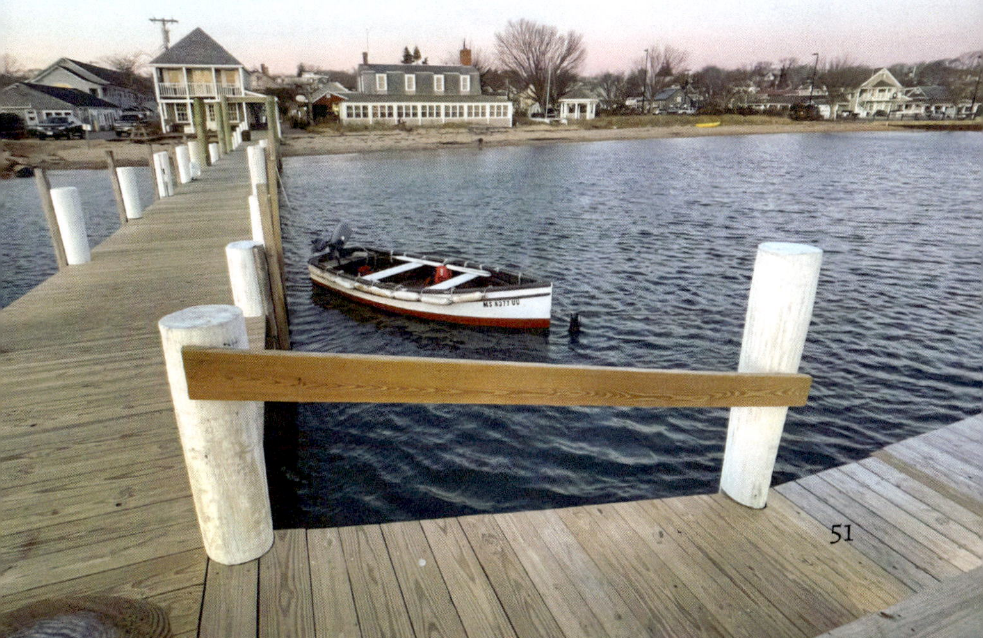

the beyond

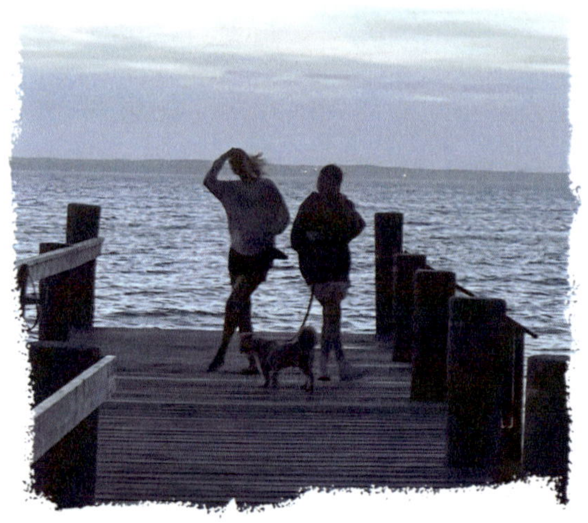

At the Cliff's Edge
Overlooking - Good Morrow
Entranced with wonder
Not wanting
This Night to leave us
Pass by way's side
Fleeing - too quickly
Haste - without reason
Beyond our reach
Faster - than stride
Time does absolutely - Nothing
Except to fly
Beyond the horizon
Where no bird can be seen
Beyond the horizon
Where no bird can fly

rendezvous

Chance encounter
Rendezvous
When we met
Wind was gentle
Birds standing by
Surf was mellow
High was the tide
She always speaks
Whispering sigh
Gentle persuasion
Set your feet
Take my hand
Close your eyes
Take a deep breath
Hold it
Until you
Feel the flicker
Feel the glow
Starts in your head
Flows to your toes
Snapped her fingers
Opened my eyes
Looked all around
Only thing to be seen
Morning's Sunrise

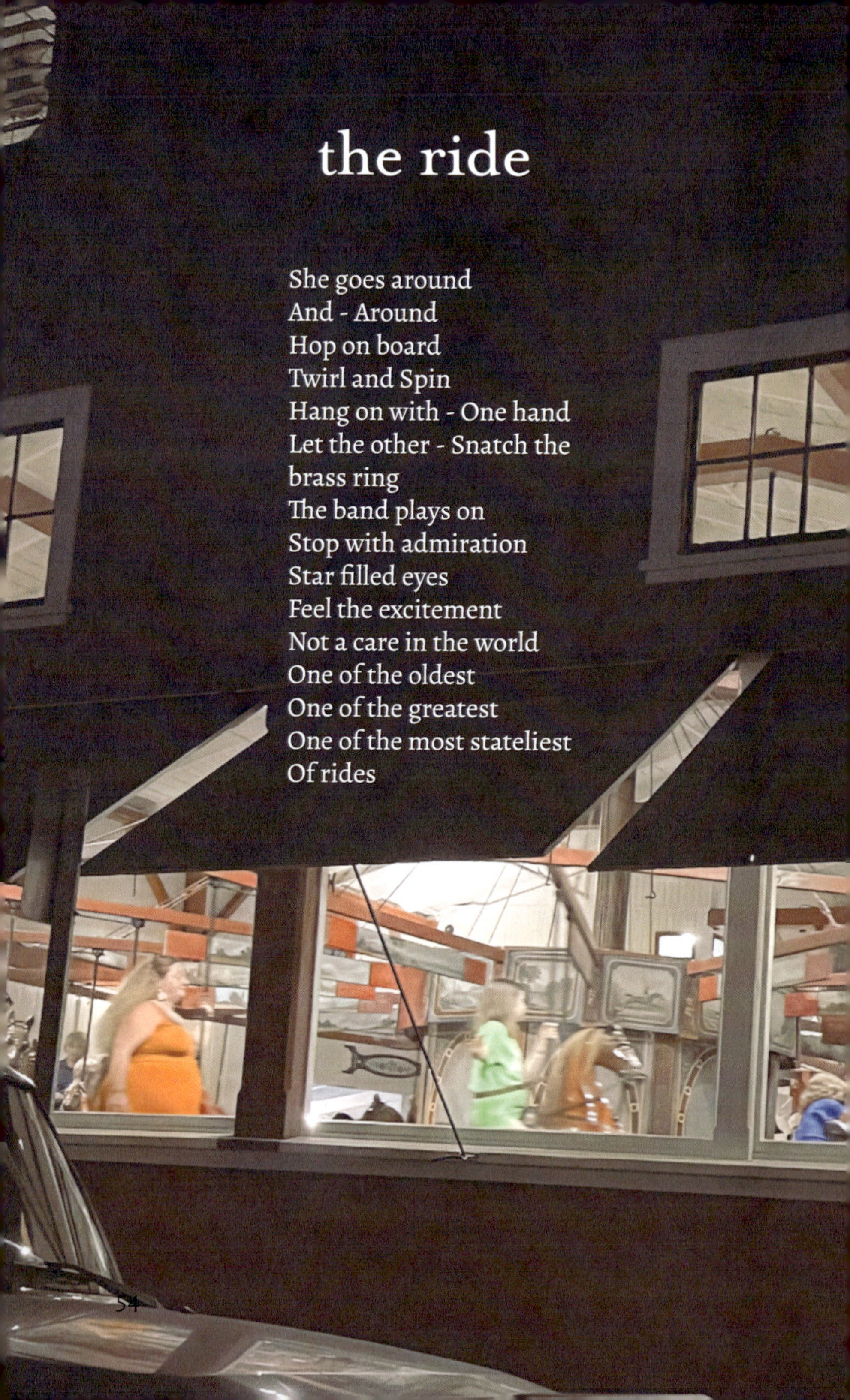

the ride

She goes around
And - Around
Hop on board
Twirl and Spin
Hang on with - One hand
Let the other - Snatch the
brass ring
The band plays on
Stop with admiration
Star filled eyes
Feel the excitement
Not a care in the world
One of the oldest
One of the greatest
One of the most stateliest
Of rides

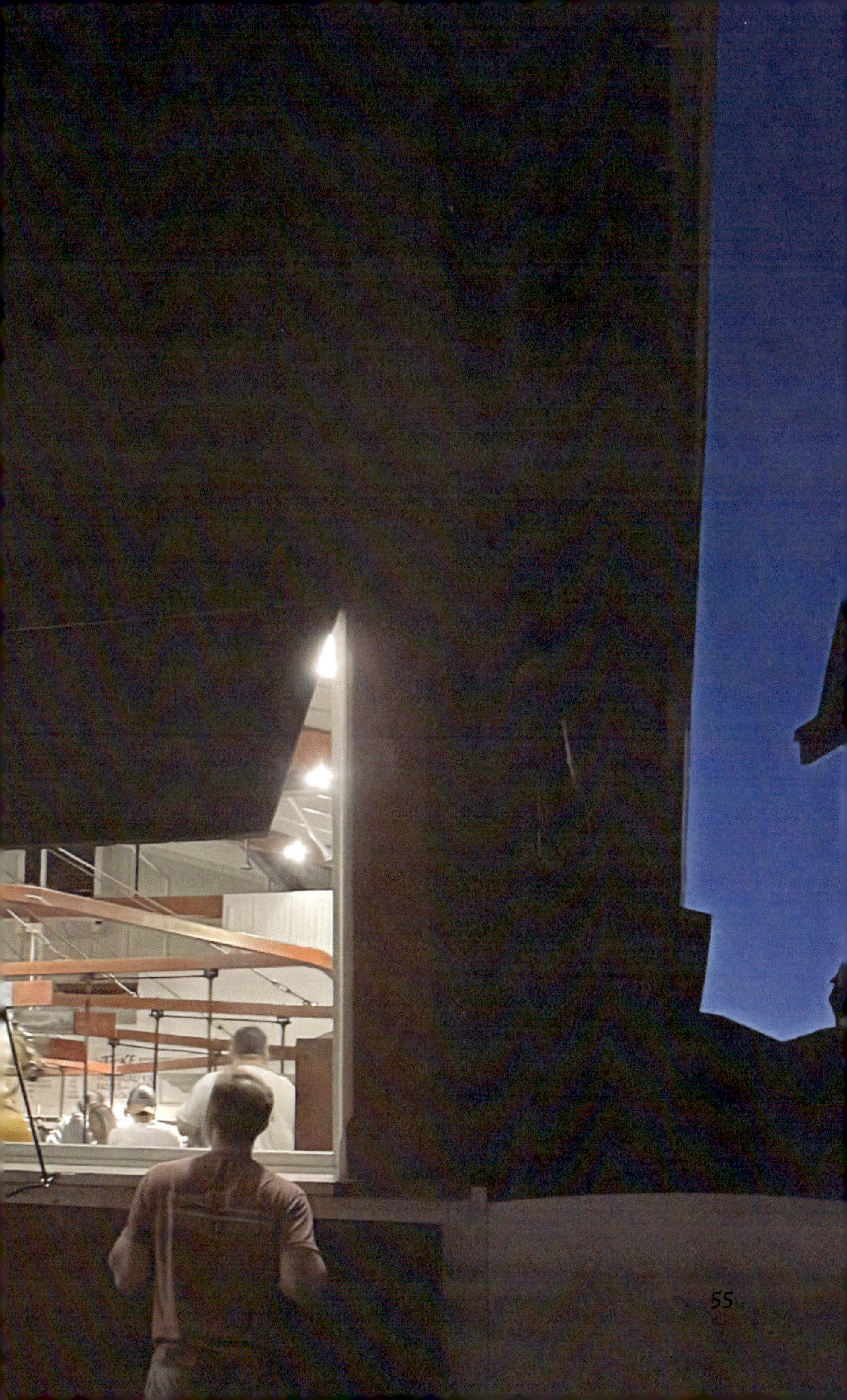

changing seasons

Catching the Last Breath of Summer
That lingers into the Fall
Cars rolling - to the Island
In the Season
Some call - best of them all
Houses - getting ready
Bottled up - winterized
No one gonna - be here
Till Spring
Shows its face
Starts to rise
Those long lines at the Grocery Stores
Gonna shrink
Like a cheap shirt in the dryer
That's what happens on an Island
When Summer has vanished
Turned down the fire
You can still hear the echoes
Calling through the fog
From those hard working Ferries
Always - chugging along

They're the lifeline to the Island
Always - weather the storm
For those who are curious
Who really want to know
What it's like to be
In the middle
Of a Northeaster's Fury
When winter
Spreads its snow
On the sands of the Sea Shore
Covering the Sound
It's more - magnificent
It's more - precious
Than a sentimental
Hallmark Card

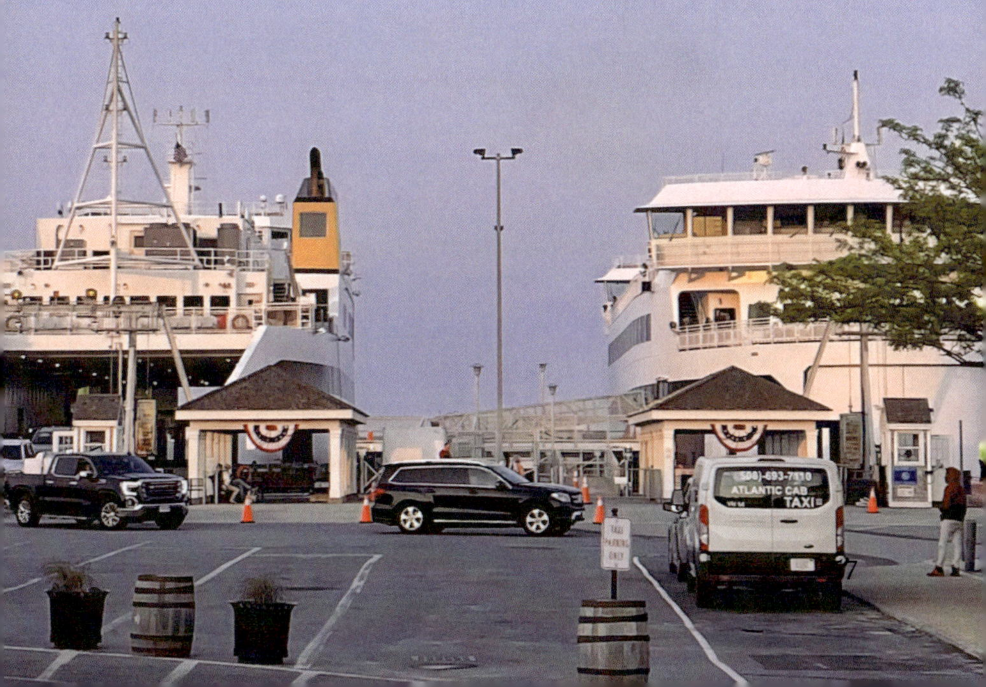

the clock

Morning's walk
At Sunrise
Everything's at Peace
At Ease
Two worlds Connected
Feel it - In the breeze
No words - Uttered
No Ferry
Beat the Clock
Precious are these moments
Time hid the Key
So no one
Can wind
The Clock

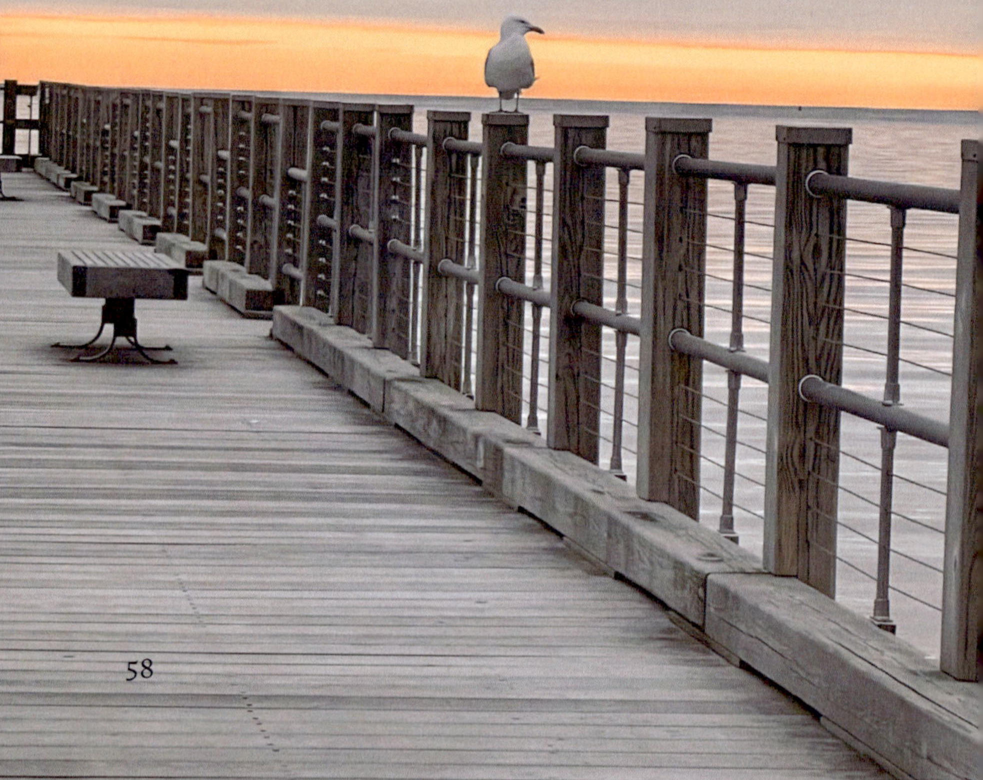

afterword

the conversion / the age of awakening

Bob became interested in poetry, about four years before publishing this book. It started by happenstance when he noticed how the followers of Emily Dickinson displayed their admiration and affection at her final resting place. Bob noticed the perpetual array of deep hearted tokens of appreciation ranging from postcards, notes, letters, feathers, stones, pens, jewelry, flowers and more left around her memorial.

His interest became more pronounced when he was a participant in a "Marathon" of reading her entire compilation of 1,789 poems at her Amherst homestead sponsored by the Emily Dickinson Museum.

He was further inspired by an event at the Emily Dickinson Museum that focused on Emily's Poems. Bob wrote a letter to the editor of The Daily Hampshire Gazette along with his poem, which was published. He became enlightened after he visited the Emily Dickinson Museum to view the exhibition, inspired by the poem "This is my letter to the World / That never wrote to Me," this exhibition showcases the powerful, global impact of Emily Dickinson's poetry. In late 2019, the Emily Dickinson Museum invited the public to contribute to a crowd-sourced project with a simple prompt: to purchase or create an original postcard with greetings to Emily Dickinson from their corner of

the world. The response was overwhelming, as hundreds
of postcards poured in from as near as Amherst and as
far as Russia. Postcards arrived from thirty-one states
and twenty-one countries, and were written in English,
Spanish, Italian, Greek, Hungarian, French, Irish, and
Portuguese. Bob's Letter to the Editor - Characterized the
Letters as, " A National Treasure."

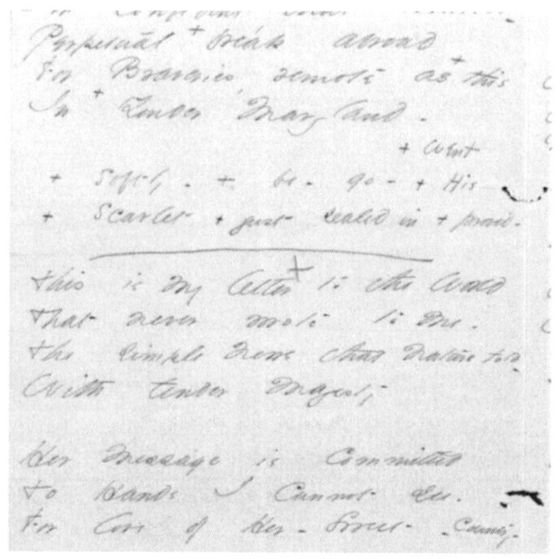

"This is my letter to the world," Emily Dickinson, circa 1862.
Courtesy of the Emily Dickinson Archive.

poems and photography

According to Bob, Martha's Vineyard is a "Timeless Treasure" that inspires from the time the Sun rises - until it sets - and on into the night. Bob is constantly searching for new meanings - new messages - new ideas that are blooming all year round. He wakes in the morning to catch the Sunrise - goes through the day and preserves moments that capture his imagination. At Sunset he follows those who perform the daily ritual of watching the Sun - Fade into the Evening Sky. All the photos of Martha's Vineyard were taken by Bob.

layout and design

Dimitri LaBarge of South Hadley, MA designed this book and was extremely helpful in all aspects of its production.

npr poetry with kwame alexander

Bob's photographs and poems were written in a method called "Ekphrastic" which means to write a poem describing a picture and more. Bob learned about this method when Kwame Alexander sponsored a contest on NPR using the Ekphrastic method. Bob quickly embraced it and found comfort in using one picture - as a focal point for a poem.

Over the past few years Bob has written hundreds of
poems which he published in Facebook Groups including
NPR Poetry With Kwame Alexander and multiple groups
from Martha's Vineyard and his hometown of Medford,
Massachusetts. His poems were well received and many
readers prompted him to compile them into a book.
Participants in this group including Bonnie Bostrom
and Melva Pawley Wharton were most helpful in their
continued support and written responses to poems
published in the Facebook Format.

And a big shout out to those Facebook people who cheered
me on.

acknowledgments

Special thanks to Jerry (Fraternity Brother) and Jane
Berman - Frank (Fraternity Brother) and Jackie Gagliardi,
Robert and Susan Penta and David Skerry - long time
Medford High School and Suffolk University College
friends to Bonni and Bob.

Hats off to Laura Dugan, Host of "Looking Back at
Medford History," who recognized Bob's Talent and invited
him to appear in her Community Access Program show
several years ago on Medford's Community Media Access
TV Station.

I want to acknowledge the encouragement from my friends
and classmates from Medford - Marlene (Boback) English,
Phyllis (Zero) Murphy, Ann Marie Jordan Christenson and
Tommy Christenson, Pat Mattie, Marilyn (Martello) Todd
and Al Morse who encouraged me to take more pictures
and do more writing.

Special Thanks to Lani Shumway for her insight and skills.
Lani and Bob are in the process of working on a similar
project.

And a big shout out to those Friends and Facebook people
who cheered me on: Gabby (MAD GABS) Melchionda,
Alex Seymour, Harry Seymour, Debra Luce, Mark Kelleher,
Lauretta Ford, Michael Mehan, Melisa Clifford, Kate
Bedard, Claudia O'Brien, Big Al Sorensen, Ed Mientka,

Aaron and Dianne Mintz, Lorraine Kieras, Mary Beth (MB) Pelosky, Daniel Sagalyn, Elaine Grossman, Anthony Piland, Mary Lou - The Love of Spumoni - Fame , Margaret Menz-Calabro, Brenda Karwin Green, Aunt Kathy Ryan, Caroline Dee Thornton, Lee Larchevesque, Joel Boone, Tomi Gomory, Lisa Straight, Craig Russell, Christine Bond, Maria Previti Spinale, Linda Gerri, Kate Gately Marini, Miranda Louise, Elaine Krevenchuk, Millicent Jackson, Cheryl Donovan, Robin from Goshen, Leigh & Bernadette Cormie, Linda Lugar, Cathy and Nick Ferrara, Diane and Kieras - Ciolkos, Dave Ciolkos, Lori and David Rezendes, Kim Deshields, Bonnie McDermott - and many others.

about the author

Bob has been married for almost 60 years to his wife Bonni. They have three children Lori, Stacey and Kim who grew up in Amherst, Massachusetts. The DiCarlo family has spent Summer and Winter retreats on Martha's Vineyard since the 80's and settled into their Martha's Vineyard home over twenty years ago where the tradition lives on with their six grandchildren Allie, Joey, Sophia, Bella, Julia and Gabe.

Bob DiCarlo is a Researcher - Teacher - Administrator and Professor, who worked at Beverly High School, The Massachusetts Department of Education, Fitchburg State University, Greenfield Community College and The University of Massachusetts - Amherst - where he retired after completing thirty-two years of public service. He presented Seminars, co-authored and authored Books, Research Studies, and Journal Articles in the areas of Organizational Development, Education and Environmental Health and Safety. He also completed his Military Duty with the Massachusetts National Guard's - Yankee Division out of Medford, Massachusetts.

He was cited by a Gubernatorial Commission for his leadership in the area of Child Labor Laws and spearheaded the implementation of the first in the Nation - OSHA Certification programs for High School Students in Massachusetts in Collaboration with the US Department of Labor's OSHA Training Institute in Rosemount, Illinois -

after he crafted an agreement with Mr. Robert McKeand, Director.

He was also recipient of a Public Service Endowment Grants (PSEG) from the University of Massachusetts which was incorporated into a a research study for the Senate Committee on Post Audit and Oversight of The Massachusetts State Legislature along with Jeffrey Sedgwick, Associate Professor, University of Massachusetts Amherst. Another grant was used to produce and conduct the implementation of the Statewide Training for The Community Right to Know Law for the entire Commonwealth of Massachusetts.

He was on the Advisory Board at Northeastern University's Cooperative Education Program and the Chief Architect in collaboration with Sid Austin, Dean, in the design and implementation of the New England Association for Cooperative Education and Field Experience (NEACEFE) .

While serving on the advisory board for the Massachusetts Seat Belt Coalition and the Governor's Highway Safety Bureau, Bob coordinated events at the University of Massachusetts, Amherst and was invited to speak as a witness, at Legislative Hearings to promote the implementation of the Massachusetts Seat Belt Law.

Bob is an entrepreneur and formed the Occupational Safety and Health Associates, Inc. which sponsored OSHA seminars for Private Sector - Business and Industry Leaders through Massachusetts.

After his retirement from teaching, Bob focused full time
on his family and business - B&B Appliance, following
in the footsteps of his Father, Joseph who taught him the
Trade. Bob worked full time at his Father's Appliance
Store in Cambridge, MA., while he matriculated for a BS
at Suffolk University and was the first Evening Division
Student to receive the Trustee Scholarship. He completed
his degree requirements - Cum Laude - in Five Years.

He was awarded a Masters in Educational Leadership from
Northeastern University as part of his Fellowship funded
by The Education Professions Development Act of 1967
and went on to study in the Doctorate Program, at the
University of Massachusetts, Amherst.

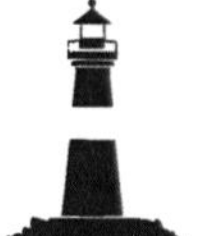

www.ingramcontent.com/pod-product-compliance
Lightning Source LLC
Chambersburg PA
CBRC090744110726
48005CB00007B/963